early Communication Skills

3rd Edition

Charlotte Lynch & Julia Kidd

Speechmark

WITHDRAWN FROM UNIVERSITIES AT MEDWAY LIBRARY

DRILL HALL LIBRARY MEDWAY

UNIVERSITIES AT MEDWAY

D1759052

Please note that, for simplicity, in this book 'he' is used to refer to the child and 'parent' to refer to parents, carers and key workers.

1 0 APR 2017

First published in 2016 by
Speechmark Publishing Ltd,
2nd Floor, 5 Thomas More Square, London E1W 1YW, UK
Tel: +44 (0)845 034 4610   Fax: +44 (0)845 034 4649
www.speechmark.net

© Charlotte Lynch & Julia Kidd, 2016

All rights reserved. The whole of this work, including all text and illustrations, is protected by copyright. No part of it may be copied, altered, adapted or otherwise exploited in any way without express prior permission, unless in accordance with the provisions of the Copyright Designs and Patents Act 1988 or in order to photocopy or make duplicating masters of those pages so indicated, without alteration and including copyright notices, for the express purpose of instruction and examination. No parts of this work may otherwise be loaded, stored, manipulated, reproduced, or transmitted in any form or by any means, electronic or mechanical, including photocopying and recording, or by any information storage and retrieval system, without prior written permission from the publisher, on behalf of the copyright owner.

Design and artwork by Moo Creative (Luton)

002-6064

British Library Cataloguing in Publication Data
A catalogue record for this book is available from the British Library

ISBN 978 1 91118 626 7

Contents

Acknowledgements

This publication would not have been possible without the interest shown by colleagues, both in education and in health. We would particularly like to thank Gill Edelman, Morag Bowen and Terry Callaghan for their encouragement and support throughout. We are also very grateful to David Eccles and Anna Cooper for their help with the resource pictures.

We are indebted to the parents and children with whom we have worked and hope that this publication will be of benefit to them and other families.

P You may photocopy this page for instructional use only © Charlotte Lynch & Julia Kidd, 2016 Speechmark

Preface to the third edition

This new edition of *Early Communication Skills* has been updated to include more activities and resources, including a new section on *Putting Words Together*. In response to feedback from colleagues, the jargon-free style has been retained throughout. There is also a new section in the Appendix which could form the basis of either a six-session programme for a parent support group or a training package for Early Years staff.

Charlotte Lynch and Julia Kidd
(March 2016)

Ⓟ You may photocopy this page for instructional use only © Charlotte Lynch & Julia Kidd, 2016 Speechmark 5

Introduction

This book is aimed at professional people working with pre-school children and their parents, carers or teachers. It should be valuable in homes, playgroups and nurseries, providing a framework on which to base activities. It will be of particular interest to people who are new to this age group or entering the specialist area of hearing impairment.

BACKGROUND

The activities were originally developed from a collection of practical ideas and approaches used by a Speech and Language Therapist and a Teacher of the Deaf working together in a Total Communication nursery (combining signing and an aural approach). It subsequently proved to be beneficial to other children with communication difficulties, and has been adapted and extended as a result of the interest shown by colleagues and parents.

The activities are based on the principle that all children learn best through play. In the authors' experience, many parents or carers of children with communication difficulties are looking for specific ideas which will encourage progress. Many of the activities in this book can be naturally incorporated into everyday routines and it is hoped that they will build on the skills which parents and carers already have in communicating with their children.

HOW TO USE THIS BOOK

The activities are divided into 10 sections, for ease of use, and cover some of the prerequisite skills essential for future language development. These skills are all interrelated and activities may be selected from different sections and worked on simultaneously, according to the individual needs of the child.

Each set of activities is preceded by 'General points', which provide the rationale for the particular activities. Targets can be discussed and agreed jointly by the professional and the parent or carer, using the tick boxes alongside each activity to plan and record the activities carried out. Parents, carers or key workers can be further involved in joint assessment through the record sheet at the end of each section, or through additional records of progress in *Early Listening, Vocalisations* and *Early Words*. These may be particularly useful for parents or carers who will observe their child in many different settings over a long period of time.

The activity sheets can be photocopied. They are intended to be distributed to parents, carers or other key workers at the discretion of the teacher or therapist, following explanation and demonstration where appropriate. They may be used in the home with parents, childminders or other main carers, and in play groups, crèches and nurseries.

Ⓟ You may photocopy this page for instructional use only © Charlotte Lynch & Julia Kidd, 2016 Speechmark

SELECTING ACTIVITIES

The activities in each section are in approximate developmental order. However, the rate of children's development, across and within different skills, does not necessarily follow the same pattern, so no age guide is given. Although the majority of the activities were written with children under five in mind, some will be suitable for older children. The selection of activities and materials will depend on the professional judgement of those working with individual children and their families.

It is important to bear in mind the setting in which activities will be carried out. Some activities might be more appropriate in a clinical or school setting. Others will be more easily carried out in the home environment. The sections *Pre-verbal Skills* and *Language and Play* focus on a natural approach to communication, which it is hoped most parents and carers will feel comfortable with. Many of the suggested activities do not require special teaching skills, allowing parents, carers and other key workers to develop their own natural style.

There are resource pictures, which can be photocopied to use with syllable discrimination activities, at the end of *Speech Discrimination*.

Several activities from one section may be carried out simultaneously in different settings, all working towards the same goal. For example, in *Early Listening: Awareness of Voice*, the family might focus on 'Symbolic sounds' (p54); the speech and language therapist could work in a more formal setting with 'Voice/no voice' activities (p61); while the teacher might try 'Listening for sounds and words' (p57).

When working with children who have a hearing loss, it is necessary to consider whether the materials suggested are within the child's range of hearing. Most of the materials suggested in this book are available in every household. The resources section in the Appendix suggests alternative specialist equipment for the listening activities which may be more suitable for using with profoundly or severely deaf children.

HINTS FOR PARENTS

Play

1   Everyday activities provide the best opportunities for learning language. Talk to your child about what you are doing throughout the day and try to involve him where possible.

2   Try to set aside some time during the day for play activities when you can give your full attention to your child. This could be part of a routine which your child looks forward to, perhaps after a drink or a nap, when he is not tired or hungry. Choose a time that suits you as well as your child. It is important for you to feel alert and relaxed too.

3   If you have more than one child, it is important that they learn to play together. However, a child with communication difficulties may be very demanding, and may respond better to some individual attention if this is possible. Try to arrange to spend some time together when other children are asleep or out of the house.

4   Two short play sessions of about 10–15 minutes may suit your child better than one long one.

5   Get down to your child's level where he can see and hear you best.

6   Keep aside some special toys for play sessions.

7   Try to put away toys which are not being used. Too many toys are distracting.

8   Switch off the television when playing with your child. Background noise or music can be particularly distracting for a child with a hearing loss.

9   Children learn best when they are interested in something. Follow your child's own interests and ideas. Don't worry if your child does not want to do what you had planned.

10 If your child shows signs of becoming fed up with an activity, leave it and return to it later, before you both end up getting frustrated.

Improving communication

It may be helpful to think about the answers to some of the following questions if you are looking for ways of improving communication. Most of the questions are also relevant to people using sign language. Do you:

◆   Give your child time to talk (or sign)?

◆   Make sure that you have your child's attention before you speak (or sign)?

◆   Try not to speak (or sign) too fast?

◆   Give your child lots of praise?

◆   Make sure that you are in a position where your child can see you?

◆   Follow your child's lead in play?

◆   Comment on what your child is looking at or doing?

◆   Repeat and expand on what your child says?

◆   Think about your lip patterns and facial expressions?

◆   Use intonation and facial expression to help with communication?

◆   Rephrase what you are saying if your child has not heard or understood?

   Ⓟ You may photocopy this page for instructional use only © Charlotte Lynch & Julia Kidd, 2016

Section 1

Pre-Verbal Skills

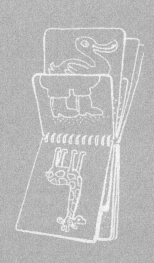

Eye Contact

GENERAL POINTS

What is meant by 'eye contact' and why is it important?

Communication between two people involves looking at each other and making eye contact, as well as talking. Establishing and maintaining good eye contact is an important social skill. Looking at the speaker's face will also provide information about language through facial expression, gestures, lip patterns and signs.

Very young children with communication difficulties may only make fleeting eye contact. This may cause communication to break down, as parents may get the message that the child is not interested.

Looking together at things in the environment is another important part of communication. The child looks at an object; the parent follows his gaze and makes a comment. This is the beginning of conversations and turn taking. These early communication skills may not develop easily in all children and may need to be more explicitly encouraged.

How can eye contact be improved?

You may need to practise your own facial expressions, to make them more interesting to look at. Emotions and feelings such as being happy, sad, angry or tired can all be exaggerated. When your child looks at you, use the opportunity to make a funny face, or show him something interesting. Holding objects near to the face and making them disappear behind the head is one way of encouraging children to look at the speaker's face.

There are plenty of opportunities for improving eye contact throughout the day: for example, waiting a second before giving your child a drink, or holding an interesting object up to eye level, although it is important to avoid battles over this. Encouraging eye contact should be as natural as possible. You do not need to move your child's face towards you. Children will look when *they* want to.

℗ You may photocopy this page for instructional use only © Charlotte Lynch & Julia Kidd, 2016 Speechmark 11

ACTIVITIES

❏ *Tracking*

Your child will learn to follow toys with his eyes. Balloons, bubbles and puppets on a stick are interesting to watch.

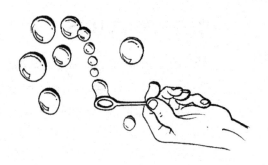

Your child may watch your face while you are blowing up balloons or blowing bubbles. Blow up balloons slowly. Wait for eye contact between each breath.

Make puppets or wooden-spoon faces disappear behind your head and wait for eye contact.

❏ *Party blowers*

Blowing party horns will encourage your child to watch what you are doing.

❏ *Coloured feathers*

Blow feathers at your child or tickle him with them.

❏ *Noisy toys*

Squeaky toys, rattles, bells or whistles can be used to encourage eye contact. Choose a toy and make a noise. Stop the noise and wait for eye contact before you start again.

❏ *Hiding games*

Wave a coloured scarf up and down over your child so that he can feel the breeze. Lift it high and let it fall over your head. Encourage your child to pull it off your head. Hide together underneath the scarf.

❏ *Peek-a-boo games*

Peek-a-boo games can be played from behind the furniture or the curtains, or when your child is getting dressed.

Ⓟ You may photocopy this page for instructional use only © Charlotte Lynch & Julia Kidd, 2016 Speechmark

❑ *Face masks*

Make face masks from paper plates and cut out holes for the eyes, nose and mouth. Use the mask to play peek-a-boo or 'Boo!' games.

❑ *Novelty glasses*

Try putting on novelty glasses and taking them off, to encourage your child to look at you.

❑ *Binoculars and telescopes*

Look through two old cardboard tubes to encourage eye contact. Longer kitchen-roll tubes can be used for telescopes. Decorating them with coloured paper will make them more attractive to look at.

❑ *Hand games*

Wave your hands and wiggle your fingers.
Hide your face behind your hands and play peek-a-boo games.
Draw faces on your fingers or use finger puppets. Wiggle them near your face and then hide them.

❑ *Hats or wigs*

Put hats on and take them off or hide your face behind a hat and play peek-a-boo games. Real or play wigs can be used in the same way.

❑ *Songs and rhymes*

'Pat-a-cake' clapping games, round-and-round-the-garden tickling games and row-the-boat rocking games are all useful for improving eye contact. Stop singing occasionally and wait for eye contact before continuing.

❑ *Ball games*

When playing games of throw and catch, wait for your child to look at you before throwing the ball, or hide it behind your back until you get eye contact. If your child is not looking, do something silly like putting it on your head or up your jumper. Instead of using balls, you can use bean bags, rubber rings or hoops.

❑ *Wink games or pass on faces*

Play winking games or make funny faces for your child to copy.

❑ *Face paints*

Using face paints, paint faces on your child's and your own face. Make clown faces, animal faces or pirate faces.

Some children may be reluctant to have faces drawn on them until they are older.

❑ *Balloons*

Blow up balloons and, between breaths, wait for eye contact before continuing to blow.

❑ *Marble run or toy cars*

Hold up objects near to your face to get eye contact before making a sound and dropping a marble or toy car down a hole or slope.

Take care with marbles and young children and ensure that the children are supervised.

℗ You may photocopy this page for instructional use only © Charlotte Lynch & Julia Kidd, 2016 Speechmark

Attention

GENERAL POINTS

What is meant by 'attention' and why is it important?

It is not unusual for young children to have a short attention span. Working on 'attention' aims to extend the time a child can concentrate on, or 'attend to', one activity. Improving concentration will be helpful in all areas of learning. A good attention span will help children understand language more easily.

As children become more mature, their level of attention changes. For example, a typical one-year-old is easily distracted. A typical two-year-old may have very definite ideas about how to play, and will be resistant to adult intervention. By the age of three, children become more flexible in their play, and can begin to give their attention to adult instructions. Some children may need help to move from one stage of attention to the next.

There are lots of different ways of playing with the same thing and extending your child's interest. Try to think of ways to sustain interest in the same toy or activity by playing with toys in different ways.

How can attention span be improved?

◆ It is helpful to remove distractions.

◆ Choose toys or materials which your child is most interested in.

◆ Playing with the same object in many different ways can help to develop attention span.

◆ Adding surprise to games will help add to your child's enjoyment and interest; for example, hiding things or wrapping them in paper.

◆ Most importantly, follow your child's lead. It may be enough simply to play alongside him, showing an interest and commenting on what he is doing.

◆ As your child's attention span improves, encouraging eye contact and allowing him time to respond to your suggestions will be helpful.

ACTIVITIES

❑ *Balloons*

Blow up balloons and let them go.

Feel the air coming out of them.

Make appropriate noises: 'wheeee!', 'whoosh!'

Throw and catch them.

Bounce them.

Draw faces on them.

Stick shapes on them.

Half-fill them with coloured water and freeze them.

Glue newspaper on them, to make papier-mâché models, and paint them.

Pop them!

❑ *Nesting barrels or stacking beakers*

Use them for counting and matching colours.

Build towers in different ways.

Roll them to each other.

Hide objects inside them and play memory games.

Sort coloured sweets into them.

Play with them in the bath; fill them with water or float them.

Use them to make sandcastles.

Wash them.

Hide them around the room.

❑ *Coloured beads, buttons or cotton reels*

Make necklaces, bracelets or 'snakes'. Sort them into colours, shapes and sizes.

Put them in pots and shake them.

Make patterns, such as red–blue–red–blue.

Make towers.

Hide them in your pockets.

℗ You may photocopy this page for instructional use only © Charlotte Lynch & Julia Kidd, 2016 Speechmark

❑ *Feely boxes*

Place an object of interest in the box and open the lid slowly. Let your child put his hand in the box and feel it. Then take out the object and play with it. Objects of interest could include the following.

◆ A glove puppet: give it a 'pretend' drink

                             give it a kiss

                             give it a hat

                             stroke the puppet.

                             (See more ideas in *Vocalisations*, p67, encouraging babble.)

◆ An apple: wash it

                             cut it into halves or quarters

                             count the pips

                             peel it

                             make apple sauce

                             make apple pie

                             plant the pips.

◆ Playdough: roll it out and cut out shapes with pastry cutters

                             make balls or sausages

                             make models (cats, snakes, birthday cakes with 'candles', snowmen, bird's nest with eggs in it)

                             make bracelets, rings, faces, insects.

◆ A bean bag: throw it and catch it
shake it
balance it on your head
hide it
throw it into a box or basket.

❏ *Inset puzzles*

Take out all of the puzzle pieces and put them back in, one piece at a time. As you are doing this, talk about each piece and learn the words or signs for them.

Hide one puzzle piece and ask your child which one is missing; or hide a piece in one hand and let your child guess which hand it is in.

Match the puzzle pieces to real objects or pictures.

Put the pieces in empty pots and shake them.

Draw round them.

Make them stand up.

❏ *Toy bricks*

Build towers or walls and knock them down.

Line up the bricks and push them along a table, like a train.

Play peek-a-boo games with them.

Bang them together.

Hide bricks of different colours or sizes around the room.

Play 'Hunt the matching brick'.

Wooden bricks of different shapes can be made into simple animal shapes: for example, cats or giraffes.

Make squares or rectangles with the bricks.

Make patterns: for example, big–small–big–small.

Ⓟ You may photocopy this page for instructional use only © Charlotte Lynch & Julia Kidd, 2016 Speechmark

❑ *Posting boxes*

As well as posting shapes into them, try playing with the shapes in unusual ways, to make it more of a social game. For example:

hide one behind your back or in one hand

put one on your head

hide one in your pocket, or down your jumper or up your sleeve

throw one and catch it

draw round the shapes and colour them in

Make towers with them.

❑ *Books and songs*

Lift-the-flap books, pop-up books, musical books and 'feely books' may be more interesting for your child, holding his attention longer. Singing rhymes and songs with actions over and over again helps children to anticipate what comes next.

Simple dressing-up may make singing more exciting. For example, wear a bus driver's hat to accompany 'The wheels on the bus go round and round'. Make finger puppets or small playdough models for familiar rhymes: 'Two little dicky birds', 'Five fat sausages', 'Five currant buns', 'Five little ducks', 'Humpty Dumpty', and so on.

❑ *Drawing pictures*

Drawing pictures of well-known songs, stories or favourite toys can help to keep children interested. 'Humpty Dumpty', 'Twinkle, Twinkle, Little Star' and *The Gingerbread Man* are quite easy to draw. Sing the words while you are drawing and colouring in.

Draw pictures of houses, buses, cars or tractors and add pictures or photographs of your child and other people looking out of the windows.

Draw simple face pictures: suns, flowers and stars can have faces, as well as people and animals.

Ⓟ You may photocopy this page for instructional use only © Charlotte Lynch & Julia Kidd, 2016 Speechmark

Breath Control

GENERAL POINTS

What is meant by 'breath control' and why is it important?

Good breath control is important for producing speech. When we speak, we control the use of our breath in a very complex way. This has been practised and perfected from very early on, through the experimental babble that young babies and children make. Children with cerebral palsy, dyspraxia or cleft palate may have poor control of the muscles used for speech.

How can breath control be improved?

There are many blowing games which can be used to help improve breath control. Blowing on the skin, blowing hair or blowing steam on a mirror or windows can help young children become aware of breath, by feeling and seeing it. At first, children may just watch. Later, they may try to copy you.

Ⓟ You may photocopy this page for instructional use only © Charlotte Lynch & Julia Kidd, 2016 Speechmark

ACTIVITIES

❏ *Blowing games*

Blow bubbles off the surface of soapy water.

Blow bubbles off toys or hands at bathtime.

Blow talcum powder off hands.

Blow feathers.

Blow hanging mobiles.

Blow boats or plastic ducks floating on the water.

Blow tissue-paper fish.

❏ *Harder blowing games*

Blow table-tennis balls.

Blow bubbles in water, through thick and thin straws; start with thick straws, which are easier to blow through.

Blow windmills.

Blow out candles.

Blow party horns.

Blow bubbles through a ring.

Blow party whistles.

Blow small toys off the edge of the bath.

Blow paint across a piece of paper, with or without a straw.

Blow a mouth organ, toy trumpet or recorder.

Blow tissue paper shapes across the table with or without a straw.

Blow bubble trumpets.

Practise long breaths and short breaths.

See the resources section in the Appendix for specialist blowing toys which can be purchased.

ⓟ You may photocopy this page for instructional use only © Charlotte Lynch & Julia Kidd, 2016 Speechmark Ⓢ

Copying

GENERAL POINTS

Why is copying important in the development of communication skills?

Copying is an important skill to learn because it involves cooperation and interaction between two people, which is necessary for communication.

Children learn language by copying what they hear and see. Early communication between parent and child begins with the parent copying the sounds or faces the child makes and making them meaningful. Games which encourage copying should help to improve observation and imitation skills which will be important for learning speech or signs.

How can copying be improved?

Join in with your child's play, and encourage him to copy what you do too. Copy your child's noises, gestures and facial expressions, and extend them to make them meaningful.

There will be times when children are too engrossed in their own play to copy what you are doing, but playing alongside your child will help to extend his own ideas.

Provide opportunities for your child to copy your everyday routines; for example, letting him have a cloth to help you wipe the table.

Ⓟ You may photocopy this page for instructional use only © Charlotte Lynch & Julia Kidd, 2016 Speechmark ◐

EARLY COPYING

❑ *Toy bricks*

Start by copying what your child does. For example, if he bangs two toy bricks together, you do the same. If he has difficulty, take his hands and help him bang the bricks together. Then try to extend the play and see if your child copies you: for example, lift the bricks high in the air and bang them together.

❑ *Early pretend play*

> **You will need:**
> ◆ two plastic cups
> ◆ two hats
> ◆ two pairs of sunglasses.

First, copy your child's play. If he puts a hat on, you do the same with the other one. Later, see if your child will copy your actions; for example, drinking from a 'pretend' cup or putting sunglasses on.

❑ *Copying faces and sounds*

Make funny faces in the mirror and encourage your child to copy you. Copy any faces that he makes.

Make funny sounds. Vowel sounds and babble, such as 'ahhhh/oo and ma-ma-ma/ba-ba-ba', are the easiest to start with. If you are using a visual system, such as cued speech, cued articulation or visual phonics, this is a good opportunity to use it for copying early sounds.

Copying sounds should not be too formal. Try to find sounds or faces which amuse your child. Respond to any sounds your child makes and copy them.

Copying games using phonic systems in pre-schools and Early Years, such as Jolly Phonics, can also be used.

❑ *Dolls and teddies*

There are many ways of encouraging copying by playing with dolls and teddies. You could have a doll or teddy each, or play with the same one together.

Pretend to feed them and give them a drink.

Make them jump, run or turn somersaults.

Dress and undress them and put them to bed.

Wash them and brush their teeth.

Ⓟ You may photocopy this page for instructional use only © Charlotte Lynch & Julia Kidd, 2016 Speechmark Ⓢ

Give them a bath.

Give them a kiss or a hug.

Sit them on a toy car.

Hide them.

❑ *Small rubber ring or plastic rings on a stick*

Roll the ring.

Spin it round.

Balance it on your head.

Put it round your wrist/arm/ankle/feet.

Pretend that it is a steering wheel and you are driving a car.

❑ *Beads, pegs and bricks*

Copy patterns (red–blue–red–blue).

Copy towers or bridges.

Match shapes and colours.

Copy patterns and shapes on a peg board.

Copy simple models made from building bricks.

COPYING ACTIONS

❑ *'Simon says' games*

Encourage the copying of actions, for example:

Simon says, "Clap your hands."

Simon says, "Wave your hands."

Simon says, "Shake your head."

Simon says, "Touch your nose."

Simon says, "Stick out your tongue."

Join in the actions as you say them so that your child can copy you.

ⓟ You may photocopy this page for instructional use only © Charlotte Lynch & Julia Kidd, 2016 Speechmark

❏ *Follow my leader*

This game is easier with more than one child, in a large space, but it can be done in the home too. Everyone follows the leader's actions, for example:

◆ marching

◆ hopping

◆ jumping

◆ walking with hands on head.

The children could march around with a musical instrument.

❏ *Songs and rhymes*

Sing songs and action rhymes which encourage copying, for example:

'Here we go round the mulberry bush'

'Ring-a-ring o' roses'

'Wind the bobbin up'

'The wheels on the bus go round and round'

'Row the boat'

'Sleeping bunnies'

'Five little monkeys'

'Old Macdonald'.

COPYING SIGNS

Model simple signs – such as ball, car, cake – and encourage copying. Some children may need encouragement to make signs themselves. You may need to make the sign on their hand or take their hands and make the sign together.

Turn Taking

GENERAL POINTS

Why is learning to take turns important for communication?

Communication involves listening, waiting and taking turns. Two people having a conversation take turns to speak, gesture and make eye contact. If two people talk at once, communication breaks down.

Turn taking begins very early, long before children learn to talk. Parents respond to sounds which their baby makes, and the baby repeats the sound again. This results in a 'conversation' where the two speakers listen to each other and take their turn.

It should be encouraged early on to help develop an understanding of the rules of conversational turn taking as well as encouraging good behaviour.

How can turn taking be improved?

Many young children find it difficult to learn to share, wait and take turns. These skills should be encouraged early on, to develop an understanding of the rules of conversational turn taking as well as promoting good standards of behaviour. The rules of turn taking and sharing must be clear and firm.

Turn taking can be encouraged throughout the day. To begin with, encourage turn taking when you are alone with your child. It is much harder for young children to share with brothers, sisters and friends of a similar age.

Your child must understand the language (either signed or spoken) for turn taking: for example, 'my turn' or 'your turn'. If your child is reluctant to take turns, let him have two turns for every one you have. Give lots of praise when your child has shared well and waited for a turn. Encourage children to thank each other for taking turns.

Ⓟ You may photocopy this page for instructional use only © Charlotte Lynch & Julia Kidd, 2016 Speechmark

EARLY TURN TAKING

If your child is reluctant to give up one toy, offer him another one, and let him have it only when the first one is returned. This helps your child to learn how to give and take.

❑ *Balls and bean bags*

Sit opposite your child and throw balls or bean bags to each other. Try this with brothers, sisters and friends.

❑ *Wind-up toys or cars*

Send wind-up toys backwards and forwards to each other across a table, or take turns to roll toy cars towards each other.

❑ *Posting boxes*

Take turns to post a shape in the box.

❑ *Skittles and ball*

Take turns to roll the ball and knock down the skittles.

❑ *Pop-up toys*

Take it in turns to press the button to make Jack-in-the-box jump up or a pop-up rocket take off.

❑ *Rings on a stick*

Take turns to put the next ring on the stick. You could pretend to put the wrong one on.

❑ *Lift-the-flap books*

Take turns to lift the flap. Remind the children whose turn it is next before you turn the page.

℗ You may photocopy this page for instructional use only © Charlotte Lynch & Julia Kidd, 2016 Speechmark

❏ *Building beakers or bricks*

Take it in turns to add another beaker or brick to a tower. Praise children for helping each other.

❏ *Fishing games*

Take turns at 'catching a fish', using a magnet at the end of a fishing line. Let each child collect their fish in a small container.

❏ *Puppets*

Teach a 'naughty' puppet to share and take turns, and say "Please" and "Thank you".

❏ *Bubble gun*

Take it in turns to make bubbles. If children are reluctant to part with the toy after just one go, they could each have two or three goes.

❏ *Board games*

Games such as 'Lotto' can encourage turn taking. 'Lotto' games can be made at home, using photographs of family and friends.

Taking it in turns to throw the dice in board games may be helpful. Shape or colour matching dice will be easier to start with.

EVERYDAY SHARING

Children can be helped to understand about taking turns by:

◆ using an egg timer – children can see how long their turn is

◆ using a clock timer – which can be set for a short period of time

◆ being prepared to give up a toy after counting to 10.

There are many opportunities to encourage turn taking and sharing during everyday routines, particularly if there are brothers and sisters, although this may not always be easy!

ⓟ You may photocopy this page for instructional use only © Charlotte Lynch & Julia Kidd, 2016 Speechmark

❏ *Cooking*

Take turns at stirring the cake mixture.

Take turns to sieve the flour.

Take turns at cutting the pastry (encourage children to work together and help each other: one could cut out the shapes and the other could put them in the tins).

❏ *Gardening*

Plant seeds or pips. Children can take turns at different 'jobs': one can put soil into pots and the other can plant the seeds or add some water.

Sweep up leaves: one child can sweep with a broom or brush and the other can collect the leaves in a bag or bucket.

RECORD SHEET

Child's name: ....

Pre-verbal skills are essential for establishing a foundation on which to build future speech and language.

AIM OF ACTIVITIES	COMMENT AND DATE
To improve **EYE CONTACT** (p3) This is an important social skill and will provide information about language.	
Activities tried:	
To improve **ATTENTION** (p7) This is important to support the learning process.	
Activities tried:	
To promote appropriate **BREATH CONTROL** (p12) This is important for the production of speech.	
Activities tried:	
To encourage **COPYING** (p14) This is important for social interaction and the learning of language.	
Activities tried:	
To develop **TURN TAKING** (p18) This is important in social interaction and conversation.	
Activities tried:	

P You may photocopy this page for instructional use only © Charlotte Lynch & Julia Kidd, 2016 Speechmark

Section 2

Language and Play

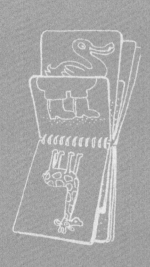

Language and Play

GENERAL POINTS

Why is play important?

Play is important for language development and imaginative thinking. There are tremendous opportunities for developing language through different types of play.

Exploratory play

Babies discover that they can make things happen through playing with toys and everyday objects. For example, when they shake a rattle, it makes a noise. In the same way, when they make a noise, they will probably get some attention.

Providing a wide range of household objects, as well as toys to explore, helps children to learn about shapes, sounds, colours and textures. In the early stages, they will learn by shaking, banging, dropping and looking at things and putting them in their mouth. As children discover the similarities and differences between objects, they also learn that different things have names.

It may be a while before children say any words but exploring toys and objects gives them the experience they will need to understand language. At a later stage, exploring different objects and materials is useful in developing an understanding of more complex vocabulary.

Physical play

Physical play and 'rough-and-tumble' games give children experience of movement and space. This will help them develop an understanding of the meaning of action words (throw, kick, run, jump, etc) and prepositions (in order of difficulty: up, down, on, in, under, through, between, behind, in front).

Everyday experiences

Children learn by experiencing different situations. Real experiences and everyday routines are very important for the development of children's imaginary play and language.

Symbolic play

All words (whether signed or spoken) are symbols. Children have to be able to think in symbols before they can make sense of language. Pretending to give a doll, teddy or person a drink from a cup is one of the first steps of symbolic play. At a later stage, symbolic play offers opportunities to extend more complex vocabulary.

Cooperative play

Learning to play together is an essential part of early communication. Children learn language and social skills from each other and spark off imaginative ideas in play.

Imaginative and role play

Children who play 'shops' are learning about the world by acting out their own experiences. They are also experimenting with language and communication. Children whose speech and language are delayed will still need activities appropriate to their age and interest. They may play imaginatively but will need help in communicating their ideas through speech or sign.

Free play

It is also important for children to have time to play on their own and to 'talk to themselves'. This gives them a chance to experiment with sounds and language. Younger children may babble to themselves, and enjoy listening to the sounds they make. This type of sound play is not intended for communication but it helps children to work out sound patterns in their brain.

Ⓟ You may photocopy this page for instructional use only © Charlotte Lynch & Julia Kidd, 2016 Speechmark

Exploratory Play

ACTIVITIES

❑ Using the senses

Give your child experience of lots of different things to play with. A collection of safe household objects and ordinary materials is interesting for young children. Collect items such as the following:

wooden or metal spoons	plastic or paper plates
shiny paper	tissue paper
bubble-wrap	newspaper
ribbons	scarves
old pairs of tights	empty pots or biscuit tins
wool	old set of keys
bells	cotton reels
scraps of different materials	old kitchen-roll tubes
baby brush	jam or coffee jar lids
plastic bottles	cardboard boxes

◆ Keep a special box or basket for household objects which are safe for your child, and change the contents regularly so that he does not lose interest.

◆ Put the objects in feely boxes or drawstring bags and take out one at a time to explore it.

◆ Crumple up or tear bits of paper to make noises.

◆ Bang things together and take them in and out of empty pots with lids on.

◆ Cover objects with a scarf and encourage your child to pull it off.

◆ Stuff old pairs of tights with wool or other objects.

◆ Fasten ribbons to old kitchen-roll tubes and wave them.

◆ Make a wooden spoon puppet pop up from and down a cardboard tube.

◆ Make objects disappear down tubes.

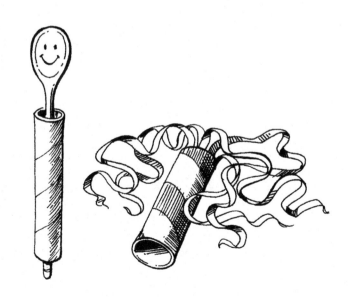

ⓅYou may photocopy this page for instructional use only © Charlotte Lynch & Julia Kidd, 2016 Speechmark

Physical play

ACTIVITIES

Many actions and words can be explored in the following games.

❑ *Ball play*

Throw, **catch** and **kick** a ball (high, low, up, down).

Throw it **into** a bucket, **through** a hoop or a basketball net.

Roll it **down** a slide.

Throw it **over** a box.

Roll it **through** your legs.

Bounce it on the ground.

Hit it with a tennis racket.

Kick it **under** a chair.

Roll it **through** a tunnel.

❑ *Boxes*

Climb **in** and **out** of boxes.

Open each end of a large box to make a tunnel to climb **through**.

Make a house with a door to go **in** and **out** of.

Throw things **into** boxes.

Jump over small boxes.

Run round a line of boxes.

❑ *Hide-and-seek*

Hide **behind** the door, **under** the table, **in** the bed, etc.

Hide things **under** the cushions, **in** a box, **behind** the curtains, **on** the cupboard, etc.

Ⓟ You may photocopy this page for instructional use only © Charlotte Lynch & Julia Kidd, 2016 Speechmark

Everyday experiences

GENERAL POINTS

What you may see as work is like play to a young child. Always try to involve your child in everyday routines, even though this may mean your work does not get finished as quickly. It will be valuable experience for your child.

❑ Helping with the washing

Children can:

◆ help to collect dirty washing

◆ remove sheets from beds

◆ help to load or unload the washing machine

◆ pass the pegs when you hang out the washing to dry

◆ put dry washing into a basket when you take it off the line

◆ sort out the clothes and put them away.

❑ Helping with certain cooking preparations

Children can help by:

◆ adding chopped ham, sweetcorn or pineapple to pizzas

◆ scrubbing potatoes

◆ shelling peas

◆ peeling Brussels sprouts (even if they don't like eating them!)

◆ shelling hard-boiled eggs

◆ grating cheese (with parental guidance)

◆ making fruit salad, jelly or sandwiches.

Younger children may like their own saucepan and spoon to 'pretend cook' while you are making the dinner, or they could wash up, using plastic pots, if you are prepared for wet floors!

Ⓟ You may photocopy this page for instructional use only © Charlotte Lynch & Julia Kidd, 2016 Speechmark

ACTIVITIES

❏ *Shopping*

When visiting the local shop, your child could buy a small item, such as a magazine or a packet of crisps. Try to make sure he knows what he is going to buy at the shop, by drawing a picture if necessary before you go.

In the supermarket, children can help to carry certain items, put them in trolleys, help to unload the trolley and pack the bags, unpack the bags at home and help put the shopping away.

You could make a shopping list with pictures or labels of some items for your child to look out for.

❏ *Outdoor activities*

Children will enjoy helping to:

◆ wash their toys

◆ wash wellington boots

◆ sweep up leaves

◆ take bottles to the bottle bank

◆ post letters

◆ plant seeds and flowers

◆ water the garden.

❏ *Bus journeys*

Even if you do not usually travel by bus, this will be an interesting experience for your child. Explain what you are going to do beforehand. Give your child the bus fare and let him look after the ticket on the journey. Save the ticket to stick in a diary or scrapbook when you get home, along with a picture of a bus.

ⓅYou may photocopy this page for instructional use only © Charlotte Lynch & Julia Kidd, 2016 Speechmark

❏ *Diaries*

Keeping a simple diary of everyday experiences will help to reinforce the language you have used with your child. Draw a picture of one activity you have enjoyed doing together each day, and write a short sentence underneath it. You don't have to be a brilliant artist. Children only need a simple outline. You may like to add postcards, bus tickets or leaflets about places you have visited.

This sort of diary will be useful for communicating with your child about things which happened in the past. Visual diaries also help with the early concept of time: for example, yesterday, today, tomorrow.

❏ *Photo books*

Children with speech or language delay may have difficulty understanding where they are going when they get in a car or dress to go out. This can cause problems when they think they are going to the park but end up in the supermarket.

A book of photographs can help to make communication easier with your child. This could include important people and places you are likely to visit, for example:

◆ a photo of all the family members, including grandparents, aunts and uncles

◆ photos of important people in your child's life (childminders, playgroup leaders, nursery teachers, friends, neighbours)

◆ photos of the park, shops, playgroup, nursery, hospital, swimming pool.

Showing your child a photograph of the person or place you are going to visit before you leave the house will help him to anticipate what will happen next, until he understands either the sign or the spoken word.

ℙ You may photocopy this page for instructional use only © Charlotte Lynch & Julia Kidd, 2016 Speechmark

Symbolic play

ACTIVITIES

❏ *Matching objects*

You will need a collection of familiar objects, including two identical objects (such as two cups). See if your child can find the two matching objects. If he can do this, match real objects to toy objects (for example, a real cup and a toy cup).

❏ *Matching objects to pictures*

> **You will need:**
> ◆ a first picture book with one picture on each page or picture cards
> ◆ objects to match the pictures.

Look at the book together and find the objects around the house to match the pictures. Or match a collection of objects to picture cards. Visual symbols or sign graphics can also be used for matching games.

❏ *Tea parties*

Plastic tea sets are useful for 'pretend' parties, but they are not essential.

◆ Stick magazine pictures of food on paper plates.

◆ Have a tea party with either real or 'pretend' food.

◆ Let your child offer real or 'pretend' food to everyone in the family.

◆ Have a teddy bears' picnic either in the house or outside.

Ⓟ You may photocopy this page for instructional use only © Charlotte Lynch & Julia Kidd, 2016 Speechmark

❑ *Large doll play*

Using dolls or teddies, pretend to:

◆ dress them, wash them and feed them

◆ wash their clothes and hang them out to dry

◆ take them for a walk in a toy pram or pushchair

◆ make a bed from a cardboard box.

❑ *Miniature toy play*

Dolls' house and furniture

◆ Match the toy furniture to real furniture.

◆ Match the dolls to pictures or photographs of the family.

◆ Cut out catalogue pictures of furniture and stick them in a scrapbook.

◆ Make a house from four old shoe boxes. Sort the toy furniture into different rooms.

◆ Make the dolls go to sleep or wake up: say or sign "Good morning" or "Night night".

◆ Give the dolls 'pretend' food.

◆ Brush their hair, dress or undress them.

◆ Give them a bath.

Zoo animals

◆ Make animal enclosures from building bricks.

◆ Make 'pretend' rocks, caves or rivers with coloured bricks.

◆ Give animals a ride on a toy train.

◆ Put them on a boat in the water, or wash them at bathtime.

◆ Feed the animals 'pretend' food (play 'matching the food to the animal').

◆ Make kangaroos hop, penguins waddle, monkeys climb, seals swim, bears growl, lions roar.

◆ Sort toy animals into groups.

◆ Match them to pictures.

◆ Draw them.

❏ *Farm animals*

◆ Match the animals to pictures.

◆ Sort the animals into families.

◆ Learn the animal sounds, such as 'moo' and 'woof'.

◆ Hide the animals around the room or in your hand.

◆ Make the animals jump or run.

◆ Give them a ride in a toy tractor or trailer.

Ducks or hens

Use a small box or basket for a nest and put 'pretend' eggs in it (building bricks will do, or small chocolate eggs). Sing 'Five little ducks'.

Horses

Build stables, fields or fences using bricks. They only have to be a simple square of bricks. Make a horse jump over the fence, and give a small doll or teddy a ride. Sing 'Horsey, horsey, don't you stop'.

Pigs

An empty matchbox can be a 'pretend' trough for the pig to eat out of. Make a pigsty using bricks or an old box. Give the pig a wash and make it go to sleep. Say the rhyme, 'This little piggy went to market'.

Cows

Make a toy cow eat grass. Pretend the cow has lost her calf. Sing 'Hey diddle diddle' and pretend to make the cow jump over the moon.

Sheep

Make up a story about a sheep in a field which escapes through a gap in the fence, and meets all the other animals. Sing 'Baa baa, black sheep'.

Make the animals talk to each other: for example, "Hello", "Bye bye" or "What's your name?"

Ⓟ You may photocopy this page for instructional use only © Charlotte Lynch & Julia Kidd, 2016 Speechmark

Cooperative play

ACTIVITIES

❑ *Helping each other*

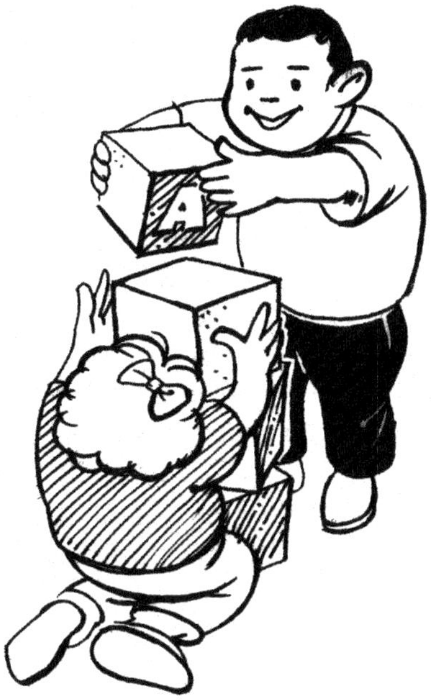

Do a floor puzzle together.

Build a tower together with large bricks.

Thread beads to make a necklace; one person can choose the beads while the other threads them.

Make 'pretend' cakes or food with playdough or plasticine to cook in a 'pretend' oven for a party. One child rolls out, the other puts it in tins and then in the oven. Others can set the table for the party.

Sand and water play: one child can hold a funnel in a bottle while the other pours in sand or water.

One child can hold a basket or bucket while the other tidies up bricks or toys.

❑ *Painting, colouring or gluing*

Children can help each other make large models or pictures, for example:

- painting a large box together
- making potato prints or fingerprints on a long piece of paper
- covering a large box with scraps of tissue paper
- colouring in a large picture.

❑ *Marble game*

Stick an old cardboard kitchen-roll tube to the table. One child can roll marbles through the tube. The other can catch the marbles in a pot as they roll out of the tube and off the table at the other end.

> Take care with young children to ensure that they do not put marbles in their mouth.

You may photocopy this page for instructional use only © Charlotte Lynch & Julia Kidd, 2016 Speechmark

Imaginative and role play

ACTIVITIES

❑ *Boxes*

Collect large boxes for your child to climb in and out of. Boxes can become houses, boats, trains, cars, rockets and anything else your child wants them to be.

❑ *Chairs and tables*

Chairs lined up one behind the other can be trains. Simple 'tickets' and 'flags' can be made from scraps of paper. Children can have drinks and a snack in the 'buffet car'.

Houses or dens can be made using chairs, tables, pillows and blankets. They can also be boat cabins, buses or train carriages.

❑ *Shops*

A small table or upside-down box will make a good shop counter.

Make an 'OPEN/CLOSED' sign and take it in turns to be the customer and the shopkeeper.

Act out the song 'Five currant buns in a baker's shop', using cardboard cut-outs, real buns or simply playing bricks for 'pretend' buns. Favourite toys can buy a bun too.

Children can act out hospitals, hairdressers or cafés in similar ways.

❑ *Songs and stories*

Children can dress up as characters in well-known songs and stories and act them out or use props. For example, a teddy, an old box, boots and a colander for stories like *Whatever Next?* by Jill Murphy. There are lots of other songs and stories to act out, for example: 'There was a princess long ago', 'Jack and Jill went up the hill', 'Humpty Dumpty', *Goldilocks and the Three Bears* or *The Three Little Pigs*.

 You may photocopy this page for instructional use only © Charlotte Lynch & Julia Kidd, 2016

RECORD SHEET

Child's name: ....

Play is important for language development and imaginative thinking.

AIM OF ACTIVITIES	COMMENT AND DATE
EXPLORATORY PLAY (p35) To provide experience of a variety of materials using all the senses. Activities tried:	
PHYSICAL PLAY (p36) To develop understanding of vocabulary linked to movement and space. Activities tried:	
EVERYDAY EXPERIENCES (p37) To experience a variety of everyday routines. Activities tried:	
SYMBOLIC PLAY (p40) To realise that one object can represent another and, at a later stage, to elaborate and extend children's language. Activities tried:	
COOPERATIVE PLAY (p43) To develop language and social skills. Activities tried:	

continued

You may photocopy this page for instructional use only © Charlotte Lynch & Julia Kidd, 2016 Speechmark

AIM OF ACTIVITIES	COMMENT AND DATE
IMAGINATIVE AND ROLE PLAY (p36) To experiment with language and communication by acting out different scenarios.	
Activities tried:	

P You may photocopy this page for instructional use only © Charlotte Lynch & Julia Kidd, 2016 Speechmark

Section 3

Early Listening: Awareness of Sound

Early Listening: Awareness of Sound

GENERAL POINTS

What is meant by 'awareness of sound' and why is it important?

Before children can understand the complex sounds of speech and language, they need to develop an awareness of the sounds around them. Through the exploration of a variety of different objects, children gradually learn to connect sounds to different actions and objects.

Babies are normally most interested in the sound of the human voice. However, for children with a severe or profound hearing loss, this may not be the case in the early stages. They may first need to understand that sound exists, and may feel the vibrations through their body before they are aware of sound through their ears.

How can awareness of sound be improved?

Introduce the word or sign for 'noisy' and 'quiet'. If your child makes a loud noise during play, cover your ears or make a sign to show that it is noisy.

Draw attention to things in your child's environment which can be both heard and felt, such as the washing machine, or music coming out of speakers. Give your child lots of experience of different sounds and vibrations.

Listening to the sounds around you can be a part of everything you do together. Point out noises inside and outside the house, for example:

◆ doors banging
◆ telephone ringing
◆ doorbell ringing
◆ running water
◆ traffic
◆ microwave oven beeping
◆ aeroplane
◆ washing machine
◆ computer games
◆ dogs barking
◆ birds singing.

P You may photocopy this page for instructional use only © Charlotte Lynch & Julia Kidd, 2016 Speechmark

How to encourage children to wear their hearing aids and cochlear implants

For children who need to wear hearing aids or cochlear implants, it is crucial for their spoken language development that they keep them in for all of their waking hours. However, some young children may reject their hearing aids, or pull them out frequently, and it can require a lot of patience to persevere.

◆ To start with, put hearing aids in when you have time to give your child special attention for short periods.

◆ Have a special box of toys for hearing aid times.

◆ Make the sounds pleasant and interesting to listen to, such as singing, xylophone, music, sound-making toys.

◆ When your child pulls the aids out, keep a blank face, do not show that you are feeling frustrated and calmly put them back in.

◆ Keep your child's hands busy with a two-handed activity, such as clapping hands, building bricks or rolling playdough, so he does not have a free hand to pull the aids out.

◆ Build up time slowly, starting with a few minutes several times a day if he is resistant.

◆ Try to avoid battles over the hearing aids.

◆ If your child persists in refusing to wear hearing aids, you may need a more structured approach.

◆ Try just two short sessions a day and build up to longer periods gradually.

◆ Give prior warning that it is 'hearing aid time' using a sign or picture symbol, with a reward, such as a game or a favourite toy, for when the hearing aids are on.

◆ Try using stickers and reward charts.

◆ Decorate the hearing aid equipment with permission from the hospital (see Pimp my hearing aids at https://pimpmyhearingaids.wordpress.com or www.ndcs.org.uk/family_ support/audiology/decorating_and.html).

◆ Put hearing aid equipment on dolls or teddies.

◆ Try some of the sound activities in this section such as 'Wake up teddy' or ones in section 6 *Auditory Discrimination* such as 'Copying musical rhythms'.

Ⓟ You may photocopy this page for instructional use only © Charlotte Lynch & Julia Kidd, 2016 Speechmark

Exploring sound

ACTIVITIES

Provide lots of experience of different sounds and vibrations. Keep a box of noisy toys hidden away for special listening times.

❑ *Things to bang*

◆ Wooden spoons or saucepan lids and a metal spoon

◆ Old jam jar lids or empty biscuit tins

◆ Toy drum or tambourine

Put 'hundreds and thousands' (sugar sprinkles) on top of a biscuit tin and watch them moving as you bang on the tin. Try other small objects such as buttons, small pieces of tissue paper, or uncooked rice and pasta.

> Remember to put small objects out of the reach of children when they are not being supervised.

❑ *Things to blow*

Blow whistles/mouth organs/musical balloons/recorders/toy trumpets.

Musical balloons make a sound as the air comes out. Let your child feel the air coming out of the blower at the same time as hearing the sound.

❑ *Things to shake*

Sound-shakers can be made by putting small objects inside old pots or tins, and shaking them to make a noise. These can be felt as well as heard. Rice, lentils and dried peas or pasta may be used if tins are firmly sealed with sticky tape. Tins filled with screw-on bottle tops and corks will make different sounds. Plastic containers will allow your child to see the movement inside as well as feel it.

You could put small objects of interest, such as a small toy car or coloured ball, inside the shakers so that your child can open them and find out what is making the noise.

Ⓟ You may photocopy this page for instructional use only © Charlotte Lynch & Julia Kidd, 2016 Speechmark

Responding to sound

Write down in the table below any sounds you think your child responds to, for example: telephone, doorbell, whistling, banging and singing. Some sounds will be easier to hear than others and will help build up a picture of the sounds your child enjoys or hears. This will be useful if you are not sure what sounds your child can hear. For older children, see if they respond to sounds by throwing a brick in a box when you say 'Go!' or gradually make quieter speech sounds for them to listen and respond to.

SOUNDS MY CHILD RESPONDS TO

Date	Sound

You may photocopy this page for instructional use only © Charlotte Lynch & Julia Kidd, 2016 Speechmark

Some children may not always acknowledge a sound by turning because of more complex needs. It is important to recognise and record the ways in which they show awareness of sound through blinking, stilling or smiling before they look for the source of sound.

Sound	Responses to sound							
	Looks for sound with eyes	Blinks	Smiles or laughs	Facial expression	Body movement	Startles	Looks for sound with eyes	Turns to sound
Bells								
Drum								
Mouth organ								
Whistle								
Squeaky toy								
Triangle								
Rattle								
Musical wind-up toy								
Bubble-wrap								
Rustling paper								
Singing voice								
Clicking tongue								
Other environmental sounds (dog barking, microwave oven beeping, telephone ringing, etc)								

Ⓟ You may photocopy this page for instructional use only © Charlotte Lynch & Julia Kidd, 2016 Speechmark

Sound/no sound

ACTIVITIES

❏ *Exploring sound and silence*

As your child's listening skills improve, he will learn to tell the difference between sound and silence. It is important for your child to explore silent things as well as noisy things.
A collection of both noisy and silent toys could include:

◆ a rattle

◆ a teddy or glove puppet

◆ a squeaky toy

◆ a rag doll or other soft toy

◆ an alarm clock (clocks which vibrate are available for deaf children).

Take toys out of a box one at a time, and let your child play with them. Draw your child's attention to things which are noisy and those which do not make a sound, using gesture or sign to help if necessary.

For example, a glove puppet could:

◆ play with a rattle very quietly or bang and shake it to make a noise

◆ go to sleep and wake up when the alarm clock rings or vibrates.

❏ *Sound-shakers*

You will need four small tins with lids, and a few small objects to put inside them.

1   Put a small object in two of the tins and leave the other two empty.

2   Shake one of the tins and see if your child can tell you whether it makes a noise or not. You may need to use sign or gesture.

3   Give the tin to your child to shake, and let him open it to see if there is anything inside.

Learning to tell the difference between sound and silence will help children to learn that sound exists. Games which encourage children to listen for a sound and respond to it will be useful for all children who need to develop their listening skills.

Ⓟ You may photocopy this page for instructional use only © Charlotte Lynch & Julia Kidd, 2016   Speechmark

❏ Jack-in-the-box

Let your child climb into a large cardboard box or laundry basket. Bang on a drum or an old biscuit tin and show him how to jump up like a Jack-in-the-box when you make the noise. Your child may need to see you making the sound to start with, and may need some encouragement to wait for the next sound before jumping up again. Start with a loud sound, and gradually use quieter and quieter sounds for your child to listen to.

❏ Come out of the house

Make a large box into a house with cut-out windows and a door, or use a playhouse. Make a sound for your child to listen to from inside the house. When he hears the sound, he could come out through the door.

❏ Stepping stones

Use cushions or small boxes to make stepping stones across the room. Choose a sound for your child to listen to, such as a drum beat or a whistle. Every time you make a sound, your child should jump to the next stepping stone.

❏ Follow the footsteps

Make several pairs of cardboard feet, and make a trail around the room. Every time you make a sound, your child should put a foot on one footprint, so that he slowly moves across the footsteps from one end of the room to another.

The four games above will work well with pairs of children, when one can make the sound and the other carries out the actions.

❏ Wake up teddy

Hide a teddy bear with a scarf or under a blanket and pretend that he is asleep. Wake him up with a musical sound. Take turns to wake him up with a sound.

Make teddy jump or walk to a sound, and stop or fall down when the sound stops.

Stop/start

ACTIVITIES

These games may work well with groups of children.

❏ *Soldiers*

1   March around the room together, banging a drum or an empty tin. When you stop making a noise, stop marching, and stand up straight like a soldier.

2   Once your child has got the idea, just bang the drum and let him do the marching!

3   Finally, keep the drum out of his sight, so that he is listening rather than watching.

❏ *Listening to music*

Play some music and let your child listen to it. He may also like to feel the vibrations of the music by putting his hands on the speakers or by sitting on a hard surface next to the speakers. Make a doll or teddy dance to the music and fall down when the music stops.

Dance or rock to the music and encourage your child to do the same until the music stops. Alternatively, your child could sit on a cushion, pretend to go to sleep or put on a hat when the music stops.

❏ *Pass the bean bag*

A group of children can pass round a bean bag. When the music stops, the child holding the bean bag has to perform an action, such as putting on a hat or scarf, walking round the circle with the bean bag on his head, or throwing the bean bag into a bucket.

Ⓟ You may photocopy this page for instructional use only © Charlotte Lynch & Julia Kidd, 2016 Speechmark

Locating sounds

Helping children to find where the sound is coming from is important for safety. For example, it may be useful for locating the sound of a car approaching or a warning beep. It will also be a useful skill for identifying where the speakers are in a group.

Locating sound may be difficult for some children with a hearing loss but it can be improved, particularly if the hearing loss is similar in both ears.

ACTIVITIES

❏ *Hide and seek the sound*

Choose a toy which your child can hear. It may be a loud banging toy or a quiet musical toy. Show this to your child and let him play with it for a while. Explain that you are going to hide yourself in the room with the toy. He may need to see you doing this at first. Make the sound from your hiding place, and see if he can find you by listening for the sound.

❏ *Blindfold game*

Demonstrate to your child the noise you are going to make. Then blindfold your child, or tell him to close his eyes, and make the sound on one side of his head. See if he can point to the ear in which he heard the sound.

❏ *Find the musical toy*

Wind up the musical toy and listen to the sound together. Put a cushion at each end of the sofa and hide the toy underneath one of them. Encourage your child to listen and locate the sound. Instead of cushions, you could use tins or boxes to hide the toy in.

For a louder sound, you could use a drum. For a quieter sound, try an alarm clock beeping.

As your child gets better at this game, hide toys anywhere in the room.

WITHDRAWN FROM UNIVERSITIES AT MEDWAY LIBRARY

RECORD SHEET

Child's name: ....

Before children can understand the complex sounds of speech and language, they need to develop an awareness of sounds around them.

AIM OF ACTIVITIES	COMMENT AND DATE
EXPLORING SOUND (p43) To provide experience of different sounds and vibrations.	
Activities tried:	
SOUNDS MY CHILD RESPONDS TO (p44) To encourage and identify response to a variety of sounds.	
Activities tried:	
SOUND/NO SOUND (p46) To encourage learning the difference between sound and silence.	
Activities tried:	
STOP/START (p48) To recognise when a sound stops.	
Activities tried:	
LOCATING SOUNDS (p49) To identify the direction of sounds.	
Activities tried:	

Ⓟ You may photocopy this page for instructional use only © Charlotte Lynch & Julia Kidd, 2016 Speechmark

Section 4

Early Listening: Awareness of Voice

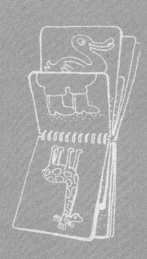

Early Listening: Awareness of Voice

GENERAL POINTS

What is meant by 'awareness of voice' and why is it important?

Children learn a lot about voice and speech sounds before they recognise the meaning of words. Listening games encourage children to develop a greater awareness of speech sounds and early words, through listening and responding in a particular way.

How can awareness of voice be improved?

Make funny sounds for your child to listen to and vary the pitch of your voice when you talk, to make it more interesting to listen to. Exaggerate your facial expression, and use all the other senses of hearing, touch and vision.

All young children learn through repetition. Singing simple rhymes and songs over and over again will help your child to become more aware of voice and rhythm of speech.

Ⓟ You may photocopy this page for instructional use only © Charlotte Lynch & Julia Kidd, 2016 Speechmark 61

Symbolic sounds

Symbolic sounds are speech sounds which are used to represent objects or actions in a meaningful way; in this case, the movement of vehicles and the noises that animals make. They are repetitive, so provide plenty of practice.

ACTIVITIES

❑ *Vehicle sounds*

◆ beep beep (car)

◆ nee-naa (ambulance or fire engine)

◆ choo choo (train)

◆ brum brum (tractor)

Choose a toy to play with, and make the sound that goes with it, for example, 'choo choo' for a train. Use the sounds in sentences, not just on their own.

Push a train along the table or floor, saying "Choo choo, here comes the train".

Push it towards a box with a hole in it and stop making the sound as the train disappears into the hole.

Push the train round a track, saying "Choo choo" as it goes through a tunnel.

❑ *Animal sounds*

◆ woof woof

◆ quack quack

◆ moo

◆ baa

◆ meow

Choose any animal sound to work on, preferably one which your child is most interested in. Use the animal noises frequently when playing, but remember to talk in sentences as well as making the noises on their own.

ⓟ You may photocopy this page for instructional use only © Charlotte Lynch & Julia Kidd, 2016 Speechmark

❏ *Sound box*

Have a collection of toys in a box with associated sounds, for example:

◆ cute puppy or soft toy (aah)

◆ crocodile (ah)

◆ tractor or car (brum brum)

◆ ball (boing)

◆ slide or aeroplane (wheeee!)

◆ bumblebee toy (buzzzzz)

◆ bell or telephone (ring ring)

◆ clock (tick tock)

◆ alarm clock (brrrrrring!)

◆ bird (cheep cheep)

◆ snake (ssss)

◆ ice-cream (mmm)

◆ car (beep beep)

◆ bubbles (pop!)

◆ monkey (oo oo)

◆ baby sleeping (sh)

◆ squeak of a mouse (ee ee)

Get the toys out one at a time and practise making the sound as you play with the toy together.

Stop/Start

ACTIVITIES

❑ *Stop/start games*

You will need:	Sounds to make:
◆ a toy car *or*	ahhhh, ooooooo, ayyyy,
◆ a wind-up toy *or*	wheeee, weeee, woooo, eeeee,
◆ a pencil and paper.	mmmmmm

Choose one of the sounds, such as 'ahhhh'.

Choose a toy, such as a car.

Push the car along the table or floor, using your voice to make the sound. When you stop the car, stop making the sound.

Variations

Draw a line on the paper when you make a long sound, for example, 'wheeee' for a long straight or wavy line, or 'round and round' for circles or spirals.

Draw patterns on the paper when you make short sounds, for example, 'zig zag zig zag', or 'dot dot dot'.

❑ *The Grand Old Duke of York*

Your child could march around the room to the song, 'The Grand Old Duke of York', and stand still when you stop singing. You don't always have to sing it to the end. Stop halfway through if your child knows the song well, and then carry on singing.

Ⓟ You may photocopy this page for instructional use only © Charlotte Lynch & Julia Kidd, 2016 Speechmark

Listening for sounds and words

An early hearing test used in many clinics is called the 'Go Test'. The child listens for the word 'Go' and responds in a particular way, for example by throwing a brick into a box. This game is enjoyed by many children and encourages them to wait, listen and respond to sounds. It can also help to pinpoint speech sounds your child is having difficulty hearing.

ACTIVITIES

❏ Listening for Ling sounds

These are sounds used by cochlear implant teams to assess listening for speech sounds across the speech frequencies. Children learn to associate a sound with a picture or an object, for example:

- ah – crocodile
- oo – monkey
- ee – mouse
- m – ice-cream
- sh – baby
- s – snake.

Cochlear implant teams slightly vary the pictures they use for the sounds. See the resources section in the Appendix for free downloadable pictures of Ling sounds.

❏ Listening for 'Go!'

> **You will need:**
> toy people and a car *or* bus or cotton reels and a box *or* pegs and a peg board *or* rings to put on a stick.

Give your child one object, for example, a cotton reel. Show him how to throw it into a box when you say 'Go!'. Every time you say 'Go!', he should throw a cotton reel into the box.

At first, use a loud voice and let your child see your face. Once he understands the game, use a quieter voice, and cover your mouth, so that he is listening rather than looking.

℗ You may photocopy this page for instructional use only © Charlotte Lynch & Julia Kidd, 2016 Speechmark

❏ *Listening for vowel and consonant sounds*

Try the same game with different sounds. Your child may find it more difficult to hear consonant sounds than vowel sounds.

Vowel sounds: ar   oo   ow   ee

Consonant sounds: b   g   ch   m   d   sh   s

Ⓟ You may photocopy this page for instructional use only © Charlotte Lynch & Julia Kidd, 2016 Speechmark

Listening for words in a phrase

ACTIVITIES

❑ *Ready, steady, GO*

Children may be encouraged to wait and listen for the word 'go' in the following games.

◆ Roll toy cars or balls forwards and backwards.

◆ Knock down a brick tower.

◆ Push a toy person down a slide.

◆ Roll a ball down a slide.

◆ Make pop-up toys jump up.

◆ Run races.

❑ *One, two, three and ... JUMP*

◆ Jump off a small step.

◆ Jump into a 'pretend' puddle (eg a plastic hoop).

◆ Make toys jump.

◆ Use a jumping spider or frog toy.

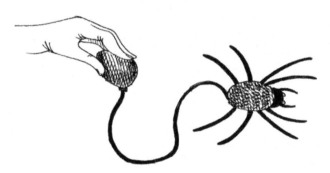

❑ *One, two, three and ... UP*

◆ Lift your child up.

◆ Throw a ball up high.

◆ Curl up small and slowly stretch up high.

Ⓟ You may photocopy this page for instructional use only © Charlotte Lynch & Julia Kidd, 2016 Speechmark

◆ Let the air out of a balloon and watch it go up.

◆ Use pop-up wooden toys, men up a ladder, etc.

❑ *One, two, three and ... FALL DOWN*

◆ Make Humpty Dumpty fall down.

◆ Make a tower of bricks fall down.

◆ Make a teddy fall down.

Ⓟ You may photocopy this page for instructional use only © Charlotte Lynch & Julia Kidd, 2016 **Speechmark**

Voice/No voice

These games help children to discriminate between spoken words and silence. Children respond in a particular way by carrying out an action when you use your voice to give the command. If you use only a lip pattern, with no voice, children do not carry out the action.

ACTIVITIES

❏ *Actions*

Clap hands.

Turn around.

Curl up small.

Play a game of 'Simon says' with or without voice.

1   Choose one of the above actions to start with; for example, 'turn around'.

2   Say, "Simon says, 'Turn around'", using a sign or gesture if necessary, and help your child to turn around.

3   Now use a lip pattern, but no voice, when you say "Turn around". Your child should stay still when you do not use your voice.

❏ *Names*

Choose an action, such as 'clap hands'.

Say your child's name and show him how to clap his hands.

Using lip patterns only, say his name again. This time, he should not clap; he should only clap when you use your voice to call his name.

It may be useful to play these games with a small group of children, so that they can learn from each other.

❏ *Listening for early words*

Your child could carry out an action associated with a particular word, depending on whether you use your voice or just a lip pattern. He could carry out any of the following actions.

Drive a toy car into a garage, or blow a horn every time you say 'car'.

Shake a rattle when you use your voice to say 'baby'.

Put a sticker on a cardboard cut-out shoe when you use your voice to say 'shoe'.

Put an apple in a shopping basket when you use your voice to say 'apple'.

Peg a cut-out cardboard jumper on a washing line when you use your voice to say 'jumper'.

Drop a boat in the water when you use your voice to say 'boat'.

Ⓟ You may photocopy this page for instructional use only © Charlotte Lynch & Julia Kidd, 2016 Speechmark

Nursery rhymes

Children can listen for speech sounds before they understand the words. Leave a pause before key words at the end of a rhyme and see whether the children can anticipate what comes next.

ACTIVITIES

❏ *Nursery rhymes*

1   Humpty Dumpty sat on a wall

Humpty Dumpty had a great ... FALL

When children hear 'fall', they can:

make a toy Humpty fall off a wall

fall off a chair onto a large bean bag or cushion

bang a cymbal or a saucepan lid.

2   The Jack-in-the-box jumps ... UP like this

He makes me laugh as I waggle his head

I gently press him ... DOWN again

Saying, "Jack-in-the-box you must go to bed".

Children can do the actions for 'up' and 'down' or make a Jack-in-the-box pop up and down.

3   Ring-a-ring o' roses
A pocket full of posies
Atishoo, atishoo
We all fall ... DOWN!

Children walk round in a circle and have to listen for the last word of this song before falling down at the end.

4   Ten fat sausages sizzling in a pan,
One went ... POP! and the other went ... BANG!

Children clap hands when they hear 'pop' and 'bang'.

Ⓟ You may photocopy this page for instructional use only © Charlotte Lynch & Julia Kidd, 2016

RECORD SHEET

Child's name: ....

Before children can understand the complex sounds of speech and language, they need to develop an awareness of sounds around them.

AIM OF ACTIVITIES	COMMENT AND DATE
SYMBOLIC SOUNDS (p54) To develop awareness that speech sounds can represent objects in a meaningful way. Activities tried:	
STOP/START (p56) To recognise when voice stops. Activities tried:	
LISTENING FOR SOUNDS AND WORDS (p57) To develop the ability to respond to specific sounds and words. Activities tried:	
LISTENING FOR WORDS IN A PHRASE (p59). To develop the ability to anticipate and respond to specific words and sounds. Activities tried:	

continued

ⓟ You may photocopy this page for instructional use only © Charlotte Lynch & Julia Kidd, 2016 Speechmark

AIM OF ACTIVITIES	COMMENT AND DATE
VOICE/NO VOICE (p61) To discriminate between spoken words and silence.	
Activities tried:	
NURSERY RHYMES (p63) To anticipate words in a familiar repetitive rhyme.	
Activities tried:	

You may photocopy this page for instructional use only © Charlotte Lynch & Julia Kidd, 2016 Speechmark 73

Section 5

Early Listening: Awareness of Voice

Vocalisations

GENERAL POINTS

Why is it important to encourage babble and vocalisations?

Before children learn to speak, they need to experiment with different sounds which will help develop control over the movements of their mouth and tongue that are necessary for speech. Vocal play is a way of exploring how to make different sounds, and is an important stage in learning to speak.

Early vocalisations are mostly vowel sounds: for example, 'ee' and 'oo'. Consonant sounds soon appear and babbling becomes tuneful: 'ba ba ba mama'. If the child has a hearing loss, babbling may stop if he cannot hear the sounds he is making. If the child wears hearing aids or cochlear implants, the babbling may start again, but may need to be actively encouraged.

How can vocalisations be encouraged?

◆ Singing, talking and laughing are all enjoyable and will encourage your child to be vocal. Sit your child on your lap, facing you, and bounce him up and down. Sing songs and rhymes and play tickling games.

◆ Whenever your child makes a noise, try to respond to it (within reason!) by either repeating the noise or extending it into a word.

◆ Children are often most vocal when they are excited or amused. Use these times to encourage vocalisations and babble.

◆ Make your voice more interesting by letting it go up and down and loud and soft, or make funny sounds for your child to copy.

◆ Give your child time to vocalise. Wait a moment before repeating a funny noise or a game your child enjoys.

◆ When your child makes a noise, reward him by giving attention and praise, or surprise him by using a hidden pop-up or wind-up toy.

◆ Make a note of any new sound your child makes and write down the date so that you can see his progress.

Encouraging vocalisations and babble

Make appropriate noises when playing with toy animals or cars and encourage your child to join in. At this stage, it does not matter if the noises your child makes don't sound like words.

ACTIVITIES

❏ *Symbolic sounds*

Use sounds for appropriate feelings and situations. For example:

- ◆ ahhhhhh
  - – Poor teddy, he's hurt.
  - – What a lovely baby!
  - – Crocodile's opening its mouth!

- ◆ ooooooh
  - – I wonder what's in here.
  - – Isn't that smart?

- ◆ mmmmmm
  - – Lovely ice-cream!
  - – That's my favourite.

- ◆ shhhhh
  - – Be quiet.
  - – Baby's asleep.

- ◆ wheeee
  - – Sliding and spinning
  - – Aeroplane

❏ *Musical blowers*

Use party horns, whistles, mouth organs, recorders, or anything else which makes a sound. If your child can hear these sounds, he will probably want to have a go. Young children may not have the breath control to make the noise but, in trying, they might vocalise instead.

❏ *Trumpets*

Use an old kitchen-roll tube as a 'pretend' trumpet to make noises through.

Ⓟ You may photocopy this page for instructional use only © Charlotte Lynch & Julia Kidd, 2016 Speechmark

❏ *Echo mike*

'Echo mikes' can be useful for encouraging children to use their voices by making noises or singing into the microphone. They are not expensive and can be bought from toy shops, catalogues or online (see the resources section in the Appendix).

❏ *Telephone play*

Talk or babble into a telephone and encourage your child to copy you. Give him opportunities to play with the telephone alone too.

Make a toy telephone from two empty yoghurt pots and string to encourage a two-way 'conversation'.

❏ *Glove puppets*

These can be a useful way of encouraging children to vocalise.

◆ Play tickling games or 'round and round the garden' games.

◆ Make the puppet sing and clap.

◆ Give the puppet a kiss or cuddle.

◆ Stroke the puppet.

◆ Give the puppet a drink and make it say "Thank you".

◆ Give the puppet a hat (the puppet could drop it, put it on upside-down, put it on your head).

◆ Make the puppet hide and then say "Boo!"

◆ Play 'wake up' and 'go to sleep' games (your child has to make a noise to wake up the puppet).

See the resources in the Appendix for additional specialist toys which can be bought to encourage vocalisations.

Lip and tongue games

These games encourage lip and tongue movements. Practising with lip shapes and tongue movements will strengthen the muscles used in speech. This is important for the development of early vocalisations and babble.

❏ *Lip games*

◆ Push the lips forward to make kissing shapes.

◆ Put lipstick on and make round prints on paper.

◆ Alternate kissing shapes with smiling shapes.

◆ Blow musical instruments.

◆ Play blow football with straws.

◆ Blow out candles, saying 'p'.

◆ Looking in the mirror, say 'oo' followed by 'ee'. Then say 'sh' followed by 's'.

❏ *Tongue games*

◆ Look in the mirror and encourage your child to copy you sticking your tongue in different positions:

upwards, downwards, sideways, around, to touch your nose.

◆ Lick lollies, sticky paper, stamps, stars, envelope flaps.

◆ Coat the back of a spoon with yoghurt and then lick it clean.

◆ Put something edible on your child's top lip (for example, a savoury spread) and encourage him to lick it off with his tongue.

◆ Use the *Mr Tongue* story (see *Resources and Materials* in the Appendix).

Ⓟ You may photocopy this page for instructional use only © Charlotte Lynch & Julia Kidd, 2016 Speechmark

Sounds my child makes

Make a note of any new sounds your child makes, and record the date below.

Date	Sound

Ⓟ You may photocopy this page for instructional use only © Charlotte Lynch & Julia Kidd, 2016 Speechmark

RECORD SHEET

Child's name: ....

Before children can understand the complex sounds of speech and language, they need to develop an awareness of sounds around them.

AIM OF ACTIVITIES	COMMENT AND DATE
ENCOURAGING VOCALISATIONS AND BABBLE (p70) To encourage the use of voice in a meaningful way.	
Activities tried:	
LIP GAMES (p72) To develop familiarity with lip shapes.	
Activities tried:	
TONGUE GAMES (p72) To develop familiarity with the use and position of the tongue.	
Activities tried:	
SOUNDS MY CHILD MAKES (p73) To record the range of sounds made over a period of time.	
Sounds made:	

You may photocopy this page for instructional use only © Charlotte Lynch & Julia Kidd, 2016 Speechmark

Section 6

Auditory Discrimination

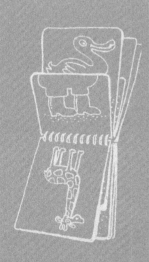

Auditory Discrimination

GENERAL POINTS

What is meant by 'auditory discrimination'?

Auditory discrimination games build on children's listening skills by developing a greater awareness of small differences between sounds. These games enable children to discriminate between one sound and another. The games in this section aim to develop discrimination skills by listening to a range of sounds.

Why is it important to improve auditory discrimination?

In listening for small differences between sounds, children learn to distinguish between differences in pitch (high/low), volume (loud/quiet), length of sound (long/short) and rhythm (fast/slow). Learning to recognise these differences is useful for understanding spoken language; it can also encourage communication through music and movement.

How can auditory discrimination be improved?

In addition to specific games, drawing children's attention to sounds in the environment and talking about them can help children to notice the differences between sounds, such as loud and quiet or high and low.

Copying sounds

❏ *Copying musical rhythms*

Fast and slow

Make fast or slow beats on a drum or an empty tin, and encourage your child to copy you. First, let him see what you are doing. Then, if he understands the difference between fast and slow, make the sound from behind a screen or chair, so that he is listening, rather than looking for the difference.

Long and short

Make long and short sounds with a mouth organ, whistle or party horn. Party horns are useful for *seeing* the length of sound. Otherwise, the sound of a whistle may be felt as well as heard. Cymbals are a good way of showing that sound can last for a long time. Encourage your child to listen for the difference between long and short sounds, and then copy you.

Loud and quiet

Make loud sounds by banging two cymbals or saucepan lids together and encourage your child to do the same. Then make very quiet sounds and see if your child can copy you. Exaggerate your movements to emphasise the difference. When your child has got the idea, make the sounds somewhere out of his view and see if he can copy them.

Rhythms

Older children may be able to copy simple rhythms, for example, slow–fast–fast–slow. Again, let your child see you doing it first. Then hide the instrument and encourage your child to copy the rhythm by just listening.

High and low

Make a low sound on a piano, xylophone or chime bar and encourage your child to copy it. Do the same with a high sound and talk about the differences. Turn your child round or show him how to cover his eyes. See if he can copy the next sound you make without looking.

Ⓟ You may photocopy this page for instructional use only © Charlotte Lynch & Julia Kidd, 2016 Speechmark

Movement

Most of the games in this section are more suitable for groups or whole classes of children but they can also be used in the home environment.

ACTIVITIES

❏ *Fast and slow*

Children run fast like a hare or crawl slowly like a tortoise when the sound signal changes, such as a fast drum beat and then a slow drum beat.

❏ *Long and short*

Children take long strides like a giant when they hear a long sound from a cymbal, or short steps like a mouse when they hear short taps.

❏ *Loud and quiet*

Children stamp their feet loudly when they hear loud banging on wooden sticks, or tiptoe very quietly around the room when the banging is quiet. Alternatively, they can jump when they hear a loud noise or sit down when they hear a quiet noise.

❏ *Rhythms*

Each child in a circle has a sound-maker, such as a pair of coconut shells. They don't all need to have the same sound-maker. They pass a sound round the circle, starting with a single beat and trying to keep the rhythm going. As they improve, more difficult rhythms can be introduced.

❏ *High and low*

When you make a high sound, such as sleigh bells, children stretch up high. When you make a low sound, like a drum beat, they curl up into a ball.

Ⓟ You may photocopy this page for instructional use only © Charlotte Lynch & Julia Kidd, 2016 Speechmark

❏ *Traffic lights*

Red: Stop (bang a tambourine once)

Amber: Get ready (drum fingers on the tambourine)

Green: Go! (shake the tambourine)

Work on 'Stop' and 'Go' first. When you shake the tambourine, children should walk or run around the room, pretending to drive a car. When you bang the tambourine once, children should freeze. Now introduce the sound for 'Get ready'. Children should jog on the spot when you drum your fingers on the tambourine. Thus amber means 'jog on the spot', green means 'run around the room' and red means 'stop and freeze'.

❏ *Hunt the teddy bear*

One child can 'hunt the teddy bear' which has been hidden in the room. Other children play loudly on their sound-makers when the 'hunter' is close to the bear, and quietly when he is far away.

❏ *Find a hat*

Children can walk around the room to one rhythm and put on a hat when the beat changes.

❏ *Pass the sound*

Children sit in a circle, each with a sound-maker. The first child makes a sound and the second child has his turn only when the first sound is finished, and so on round the circle. Some sounds are short (a bang on a drum) and others are longer (a bang on a cymbal).

Ⓟ You may photocopy this page for instructional use only © Charlotte Lynch & Julia Kidd, 2016 Speechmark

Matching sounds

ACTIVITIES

Start by choosing two different sounds to work on. Give your child time to experiment with making different sounds. Then you can copy the sounds he makes and continue to take turns.

Then hide the sound-makers behind a screen and make the noise. When your child hears the noise, see if he can match and copy it. To make this game harder, use three different sound-makers.

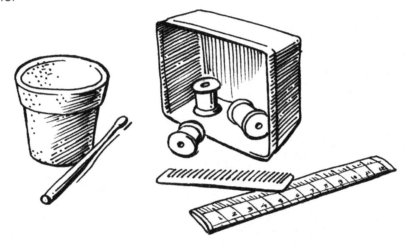

> **You will need:**
>
> ◆ things to bang (tin lids or a plant pot and stick)
> ◆ things to shake (tins with cottons reels inside or bunches of keys)
> ◆ things to scrape (a comb and a ruler, or corrugated cardboard and a pencil).

❑ Matching sounds to actions

You will need three different sound-makers: for example, a bell, a squeaky toy and a whistle.

Your child could respond to different sounds in a particular way. For example, he could turn round upon hearing the bell, touch his head upon hearing the squeaky toy, or fold his arms upon hearing the whistle.

When your child is familiar with the game, make the sounds from behind a screen, so that he has to listen carefully.

Recorded Sounds

ACTIVITIES

❑ *Noisy toys*

> **You will need:**
> ◆ a mobile phone or tablet with an inbuilt microphone
> ◆ sound toys, such as a drum, a squeaky toy or a musical toy.

Choose two or three noisy toys which your child enjoys playing with. Record their noises one at a time and let your child listen to them. Then put the toys in front of your child and see if he can match the sounds on the recording to the toys.

❑ *Body sounds*

Encourage your child to copy simple body sounds, for example:

◆ clapping hands
◆ stamping feet
◆ slapping thighs
◆ clicking tongue
◆ popping cheeks.

Record these noises one at a time and listen to them. See if your child can recognise the sounds on the recording and join in with them.

❑ *Household sounds*

Make your own recording of sounds you hear around the house, such as the telephone ringing, a door banging, the washing machine, the baby crying.

❑ *Sound lotto*

Match sounds to pictures and talk about them.

Ⓟ You may photocopy this page for instructional use only © Charlotte Lynch & Julia Kidd, 2016 Speechmark Ⓢ

RECORD SHEET

Child's name: ....

Auditory discrimination of sound aims to build on basic listening skills by encouraging a greater awareness of small differences between sounds.

AIM OF ACTIVITIES	COMMENT AND DATE
COPYING SOUNDS (p78) To listen to and remember differences between sounds.	
Activities tried:	
MOVEMENT (p79) To respond appropriately to different sounds.	
Activities tried:	
MATCHING SOUNDS (p81) To identify and match or respond to different sounds.	
Activities tried:	
RECORDED SOUNDS (p82) To identify subtle differences between recorded sounds.	
Activities tried:	

Ⓟ You may photocopy this page for instructional use only © Charlotte Lynch & Julia Kidd, 2016 Speechmark Ⓢ

Section 7

Speech Discrimination

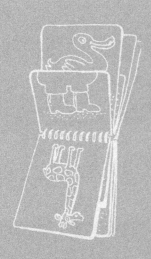

Speech Discrimination

GENERAL POINTS

What is meant by 'speech discrimination' and why is it important?

Speech discrimination activities encourage children to listen for differences between two or more speech sounds or words and phrases, building on the listening skills they already have. Recognising the small differences between speech sounds is an important step in learning to understand spoken language.

How can speech discrimination be improved?

Children can learn to recognise differences in the length, rhythm and intonation of sounds, words and phrases. In the early stages, visual clues such as facial expression, gesture, signs and lip patterns will help children learn the difference between two contrasting sounds.

Offering choices will give children everyday practice in listening for differences between sounds in a natural environment. For example, if your child wants a toy, you could ask whether he wants the 'car' or the 'aeroplane', rather than giving him what you think he wants straight away.

Children with hearing loss may always need some help from lip reading to discriminate between certain speech sounds. However, their listening skills can often be improved considerably with practice, by making the best use of residual hearing.

Discrimination between long and short sounds or phrases

Children can be 'trained' to hear the difference between long and short sounds or phrases. Learning to recognise differences in the length and duration of sound will help them to become more aware of the sounds in running speech, helping them to make sense of spoken language.

Discrimination between familiar sounds and words

Pairs of words are chosen by taking into account their contrasting visual and auditory pattern. For example, 'moo' and 'quack quack' sound very different and also look very different on the lips. Gradually, a greater range of sounds is introduced so that children are discriminating between three or four similar sounds. As they become more familiar with different sounds, they may begin to discriminate by listening alone.

Syllable discrimination

Learning to recognise differences in pitch, rhythm and intonation of speech is essential for understanding spoken language. Syllable discrimination activities aim to make children more aware of these differences.

Many of the activities in this section are particularly relevant for hearing impaired or phonologically disordered children, who frequently have difficulties with speech perception and production. The activities need to be worked through systematically, and require careful supervision and guidance from the professional people concerned.

You may photocopy this page for instructional use only © Charlotte Lynch & Julia Kidd, 2016 Speechmark

Long and short sounds and phrases

ACTIVITIES

❏ Long and short sounds

Long sounds: wheeee (aeroplane)

Short sounds: b–b–b (boat)

Play with a collection of toy boats or aeroplanes or draw some pictures and introduce the sounds. Encourage your child to make the sounds while he plays.

Draw a scene of the sea and the sky on a big sheet of paper or the whiteboard. When you say "wheeee", show your child how to put an aeroplane in the sky. When you say "b–b–b", he could put a boat on the sea.

❏ Other long and short sounds

Long sounds: oooooo (wind)

Short sounds: p–p–p (fish)

On the drawing used above, add clouds in the sky for 'oooooo' and fish in the sea for 'p–p–p'.

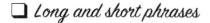

❏ Long and short phrases

Long phrases	Short phrases
turn around	run
ready, steady, go!	stop!
clap your hands	jump
run to the door	up
put your hands on your head	clap

Choose one of the above pairs, for example, 'run' and 'turn around'. Give one of these commands and show your child what to do, using signs, gestures and demonstration if necessary. With practice, your child will learn to discriminate between the two commands and carry out the appropriate action without help.

℗ You may photocopy this page for instructional use only © Charlotte Lynch & Julia Kidd, 2016 Speechmark

Familiar sounds and words

ACTIVITIES

❏ Animal sounds

> **You will need:**
> - ◆ toy farm animals
> - ◆ two old boxes or pots
> - ◆ building bricks.

- ◆ meow
- ◆ quack quack
- ◆ moo
- ◆ woof woof
- ◆ baa
- ◆ cluck cluck

Choose two animal sounds which look and sound very different, for example, 'meow' and 'quack quack'. Play with the animals and make the noises when appropriate.

Draw a picture of a cat and stick it on one of the boxes or pots. Draw a picture of a duck and stick it on the other one.

When you say "Meow", your child could put a brick into the box with the picture of a cat on it. When you say "Quack quack", he should put a brick in the other box.

Play similar games with other pairs of animal sounds. For example, you could collect pictures of milk for a cow every time you say "Moo" and pictures of a bone for a dog when you say "Woof woof".

❏ Transport sounds

- ◆ choo choo (train)
- ◆ beep beep (car)
- ◆ brummm (motorbike)
- ◆ wheeee (aeroplane)

You could do the same activity with pairs of transport sounds, hiding toys or pictures of vehicles around the room. When you say "Choo choo", ask your child to look for the trains. When you say "Brummm", your child should find the motorbikes.

Ⓟ You may photocopy this page for instructional use only © Charlotte Lynch & Julia Kidd, 2016 Speechmark Ⓢ

❏ *Action sounds*

> **You will need:**
> ◆ a spinning top (`round and round`)
> ◆ a drum or hammer (`bang bang`)
> ◆ a drawstring bag.

Play with the toys, making the appropriate noises as you play. When your child is familiar with the different sounds, hide the toys and put one of them in the bag. Make the noise associated with that toy and see if your child can guess what is inside *before* he has a look. Use pictures for your child to point to if he cannot say the words.

For other action sounds, you will need:

◆ a toy ladder (`up up up`)

◆ a toy slide (`down down down`)

◆ a plastic jumping frog (`jump jump jump`)

◆ a walking wind-up toy (`walk walk walk`).

❏ *Names*

This game will help your child become more familiar with the names of family and friends. Using very similar names will make the game more difficult.

Wrap up some small sweets or small toys and write a name on each one. Let your child help you choose two or three names for the small parcels. Mix them all up and put them in a box or bag. Take out one at a time and call out the name. Let your child give the sweet or toy to the right person.

Syllable lists

One-syllable words	Two-syllable words	Three-syllable words	Four-syllable words
cow dog bird	monkey rabbit tiger	elephant butterfly kangaroo	caterpillar rhinoceros alligator
cake pear jam milk	apple biscuit ice-cream carrot	banana tomato potato strawberry	cauliflower
car bus train	lorry taxi digger	aeroplane motorbike bicycle	helicopter
house bed chair	window table chimney	telephone computer radio	television washing machine CD player
ball book doll box	teddy baby balloon basket	roundabout telephone umbrella rocking horse	Jack-in-the-box jigsaw puzzle
hat shoes dress	jumper trousers slippers	pyjamas cardigan dressing gown	wellington boots swimming costume

There are resource pictures at the end of this section for specific work on syllable discrimination. Vocabulary should be familiar to the child if possible, and may be chosen from the syllable lists above. The following combination of syllables is in increasing order of difficulty and should be worked through at the child's own pace.

1   A one-syllable word versus a four-syllable word.

2   A one-syllable word versus a three-syllable word.

3   A one-syllable word versus a two-syllable word.

4   Discrimination between three words instead of two, which will take this one step further: for example, a one-syllable, a two-syllable and a three-syllable word.

A variety of vocabulary and activities can be used to maintain children's interest and motivation.

ⓟ You may photocopy this page for instructional use only © Charlotte Lynch & Julia Kidd, 2016 Speechmark

Syllables

ACTIVITIES

❑ *Animals*

> **You will need:**
>
> ◆ pairs of model animals or pictures.

Choose two contrasting animal words, for example: bird (one syllable) and caterpillar (four syllables).

These words look and sound very different. When your child is familiar with the words, share the animals between you and play a pairs game. Ask your child for one animal to make a pair with yours and see if he can find the correct one. Use pictures or signs to help at first.

Choose different pairs of animal words to make this more difficult, and gradually introduce a third word, for example:

◆ cow (one syllable) and elephant (three syllables)

◆ dog (one syllable) and bird (one syllable)

◆ bird (one syllable), rabbit (two syllables) and butterfly (three syllables).

❑ *Food*

Choose two contrasting words, for example: cake (one syllable) and banana (three syllables).

Draw large pictures of a cake and a banana. When you say one of the words, your child could stick a star or sticker on the correct picture.

Try to use the words in a sentence, for example: 'Put a star on the banana' or 'Put a star on the cake'.

❑ *Transport*

> **You will need:**
>
> ◆ two empty shoe boxes
> ◆ building bricks
> ◆ pictures of two vehicles.

Ⓟ You may photocopy this page for instructional use only © Charlotte Lynch & Julia Kidd, 2016 Speechmark

Choose two words from different syllable lists, for example: car (one syllable) and helicopter (four syllables).

Stick one picture on each shoe box. Your child should put a brick in the correct box, according to which word you say. Use sentences rather than single words.

Alternatively, your child could post pictures into post boxes.

❏ *The house*

> **You will need:**
> ◆ pictures of furniture stuck on card
> ◆ paper clips
> ◆ a 'fishing rod' made from a magnet attached to a piece of string.

Choose two words from different syllable lists, for example: house (one syllable) and television (four syllables).

Find three or four pictures of each word you have chosen.

Stick the paper clips on the cardboard pictures so that they can be picked up by the magnet.

When your child hears a word, he can pick up the correct picture using the 'fishing rod'.

❏ *Objects*

> **You will need:**
> ◆ two sheets of paper
> ◆ pencil and crayons
> ◆ two toy people or two counters.

Choose two contrasting words, for example: ball (one syllable) and telephone (three syllables).

Draw a simple picture of a ladder on each sheet of paper. At the top of each one, draw a picture of the words you have chosen.

Put a counter or a toy person at the bottom of each ladder. Depending on which word you use, your child can make the person jump up the ladder one step at a time. When the person is at the top of the ladder, give your child the real toy to play with as a reward.

Ⓟ You may photocopy this page for instructional use only © Charlotte Lynch & Julia Kidd, 2016 Speechmark

❏ *Clothes*

You will need:

◆ cardboard cut-outs of boys and girls with paper clothes to put on them.

Choose two words, from different syllable lists, for example: hat (one syllable) and wellington boots (four syllables).

Depending on which word you say, your child sticks that item of clothing on one of the cut-outs.

Alternatively, he could colour it in or hang it on a 'washing line'.

Ⓟ You may photocopy this page for instructional use only © Charlotte Lynch & Julia Kidd, 2016 Speechmark

Songs and stories

ACTIVITIES

☐ *Action rhymes*

Action rhymes such as 'The wheels on the bus' can be sung either fast or slow and children join in with either fast or slow actions. Songs may also be sung either loudly or quietly.

☐ *Stories*

When reading a favourite story, encourage your child to listen out for certain words. For example:

Goldilocks and the Three Bears

Every time you say "Goldilocks" in the story, your child could shake some bells, and when you say "bear", your child could roar, or take a teddy out of a box.

Three Little Pigs

Every time you say "pig", your child could make a squeaky toy squeak, and when he hears "wolf", he could blow down a paper cut-out of a house.

Three Billy Goats Gruff

Every time your child hears "trip trap", he could stamp his feet, and when he hears "out jumped the troll", he could make a glove puppet jump up.

The Gingerbread Man

When your child hears "Run, run as fast as you can", he could make a cardboard cut-out of a gingerbread man run, and when he hears "Stop, little gingerbread man", he could clap his hands or hold up a 'STOP' sign.

These listening games can be played with one or more children.

Ⓟ You may photocopy this page for instructional use only © Charlotte Lynch & Julia Kidd, 2016 Speechmark

RECORD SHEET

Child's name: ....

Speech discrimination aims to build on the basic listening skills already acquired, thus improving a child's comprehension of spoken language.

AIM OF ACTIVITIES	COMMENT AND DATE
LONG AND SHORT SOUNDS AND PHRASES (p89) To discriminate between two long and short sounds or phrases.	
Activities tried:	
FAMILIAR SOUNDS AND WORDS (p90) To discriminate between two or more contrasting sounds or words.	
Activities tried:	
SYLLABLES (p93) To discriminate between two or more words, differing in number of syllables.	
Activities tried:	
SONGS AND STORIES (p96) To listen for and anticipate words within connected speech.	
Activities tried:	

℗ You may photocopy this page for instructional use only © Charlotte Lynch & Julia Kidd, 2016 Speechmark

Syllable pictures

Ⓟ You may photocopy this page for instructional use only © Charlotte Lynch & Julia Kidd, 2016

Syllable pictures

Syllable pictures

ⓟ You may photocopy this page for instructional use only © Charlotte Lynch & Julia Kidd, 2016 Speechmark

Syllable pictures

Ⓟ You may photocopy this page for instructional use only © Charlotte Lynch & Julia Kidd, 2016 Speechmark

Syllable pictures

(P) You may photocopy this page for instructional use only © Charlotte Lynch & Julia Kidd, 2016 Speechmark

Syllable pictures

℗ You may photocopy this page for instructional use only © Charlotte Lynch & Julia Kidd, 2016 Speechmark

Syllable pictures

Ⓟ You may photocopy this page for instructional use only © Charlotte Lynch & Julia Kidd, 2016   Speechmark Ⓢ

Syllable pictures

℗ You may photocopy this page for instructional use only © Charlotte Lynch & Julia Kidd, 2016 Speechmark

Syllable pictures

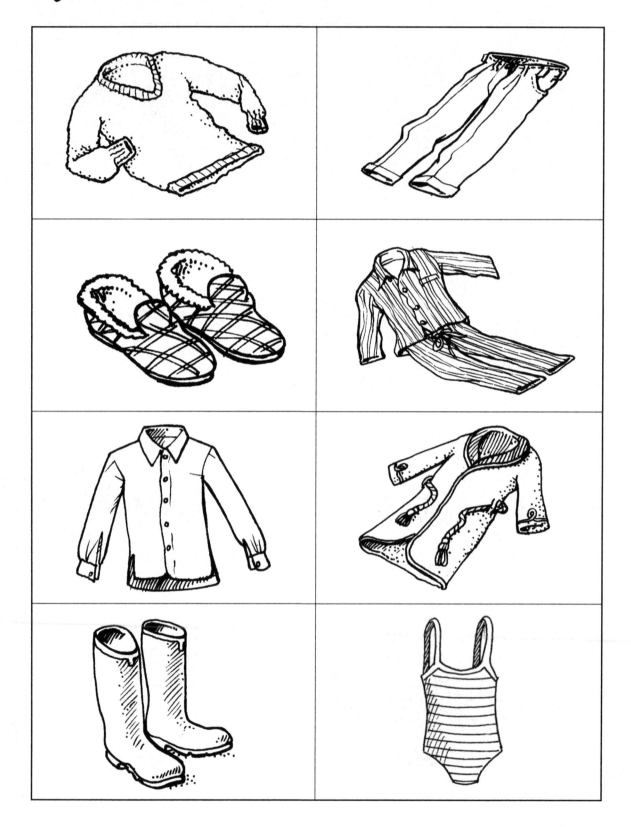

Ⓟ You may photocopy this page for instructional use only © Charlotte Lynch & Julia Kidd, 2016 Speechmark Ⓢ

Section 8

Auditory and Visual Memory

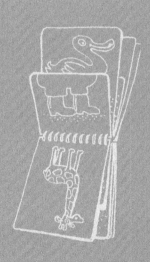

Auditory and Visual Memory

GENERAL POINTS

What is 'auditory and visual memory'?

An essential part of language learning involves remembering information which is taken in through the auditory and visual channels (the ears and eyes). Some children find it difficult to process and remember what they have heard and seen.

Why is auditory and visual memory important?

Improving memory is important for future language learning. Children use all of their senses to take in information about language. Organising and remembering this information is necessary for sequencing ideas and thoughts when using language.

How can auditory and visual memory be improved?

Auditory and visual memory games aim to improve the memory for spoken language through listening and looking. These games will encourage your child to take in and recall information. In many of the games, the skills of auditory, visual and sequential memory overlap.

You may photocopy this page for instructional use only © Charlotte Lynch & Julia Kidd, 2016 Speechmark

Hiding games

ACTIVITIES

❑ *Visual memory game*

> **You will need:**
> ◆ between two and seven different toys, such as a car, a doll, a teddy, a ball, a book and a cup.

Choose two or three of the toys and play with them. Put the toys on a table which is free from other distractions. Cover your child's eyes or show him how to turn around while you take away one of the toys.

See if your child notices which toy is missing. To help him understand, you could say, "Where's Teddy? Teddy's gone!" and pretend to look for it. Then make a big fuss about finding the teddy and putting it back on the table.

As your child gains in confidence, gradually increase the number of toys you use to make the game more difficult, or hide more than one toy at a time.

❑ *Animal hide-and-seek*

> **You will need:**
> ◆ two to five different-sized coloured barrels
> ◆ two to five miniature toy animals.

Start with two or three barrels and the same number of toy animals. Give your child one animal at a time and show him how to hide them inside the barrels. Drawing simple pictures can help remind your child where each one has been hidden. Before opening the barrels again, see if your child can remember which animal is inside each one. Give him clues if necessary: perhaps a sign or make the animal noise.

To make the game more difficult, gradually increase the number of animals you hide.

Ⓟ You may photocopy this page for instructional use only © Charlotte Lynch & Julia Kidd, 2016 Speechmark Ⓢ

Matching pictures

ACTIVITIES

☐ Snap!

> **You will need:**
> ◆ a set of 'Snap!' playing cards.

Share out the cards so that you both have five of the same picture. Put your child's set face-up in front of him. Show him three of your pictures and line them up on the table. Help your child to find the three pictures to match yours.

Repeat the game. To make it harder, turn your pictures upside-down and see if your child can match them from memory.

Gradually add more pictures.

☐ Matching pairs

Memory games can be played using only a few pairs of cards to start with. See how many pairs your child can find by turning over two at a time.

☐ Shopping game

> **You will need:**
> ◆ 'Snap!' cards or pictures of food
> ◆ a shopping basket.

Choose five picture cards and put them on the table. Say or sign which three pictures you want your child to find for your shopping basket: for example, "Give me the jelly, the sausages and the apple." Accept them in any order to start with. Then encourage your child to present the pictures in the order in which you asked for them: (1) jelly, (2) sausages, (3) apple. You may need to repeat the sequence several times.

For a variation of this game, you could write a shopping list, using words and pictures as a memory aid.

Group games

These games can be played with two or more children or adults.

❏ *Who's got the animal?*

You will need:
◆ three to six different animal pictures (for example, a cow, a pig and a horse).

Let your child give everyone a picture. Talk about it: for example, "Daddy's got the cow – moo!" Each person could mime their own picture to make it more memorable.

Turn each card face-down and see if your child can remember who has which picture, asking, for example, "Who's got the cow?" Alternatively, mix up the pictures and ask your child to return them to the correct person.

Gradually add more pictures, so that each person has two or three.

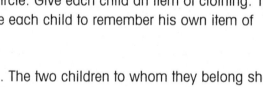

❏ *Changing places*

You will need:
◆ an item of clothing for each child (for example, a hat, gloves, a scarf).

A small group of children sit on chairs in a circle. Give each child an item of clothing. Talk about what each child is wearing. Encourage each child to remember his own item of clothing and put it under his chair.

Call out the names of two articles of clothing. The two children to whom they belong should put on their item of clothing and swap places. To make it harder, call out more names of clothes. To finish, put all of the clothes in the middle of the circle, and see if children can remember which item belongs to whom.

℗ You may photocopy this page for instructional use only © Charlotte Lynch & Julia Kidd, 2016 Speechmark

Sequencing

ACTIVITIES

❑ Feed the monster or 'Greedy Gorilla' game

Make a monster from a shoe box with a cut-out mouth and feed him items such as pictures or models of insects or animals; for example, feed him a spider, a worm and a caterpillar.

The 'Greedy Gorilla' game involves posting pictures of food in a toy gorilla's mouth (see the resources section in the Appendix). Start with one or two items and gradually increase the number you ask for, such as ice-cream, banana and burger. Alternatively, you could use real food or toy food and feed it to a favourite toy.

❑ Washing line game

Hang up a washing line, and peg items or pictures on it, depending on your child's memory skills; for example, socks, T-shirt and jumper.

❑ I went for a walk

> **You will need:**
> ◆ miniature toy animals and a screen (an old box or a book).

Start off the game by choosing one of the toy animals (a duck, for example). Say, "I went for a walk and I saw a duck." Encourage your child to repeat the word or sign for 'duck'.

Line up another animal behind the first one (a tortoise, for example) and say, "I went for a walk and I saw a duck and a ... tortoise."

Encourage your child to repeat 'duck' and 'tortoise' or make the appropriate signs.

Then add another animal (a cat, for example) and say, "I went for a walk and I saw a duck, a tortoise and ... a cat."

Put a screen in front of the animals and see if your child can remember them all in the correct order. Gradually increase the number of animals you use.

❑ *I went shopping*

You will need:
◆ a box of toys.

Put the box of toys in the middle of a small circle of children. The first child should choose one toy from the box and show it to everyone. He should then hide it under his chair. He could say, "I went shopping and I bought …" The next child has to remember the first toy and repeat what the first child said.

Then choose another toy, hide it under the second child's chair, adding it to what he has just said. The third child has to remember the previous two toys and choose the next one. Continue round the circle.

ℙ You may photocopy this page for instructional use only © Charlotte Lynch & Julia Kidd, 2016 Speechmark

Sequencing sounds and actions

ACTIVITIES

❏ Sequencing sounds

> **You will need:**
>
> three noisy toys or musical instruments, for example:
>
> ◆ a plastic cup and spoon *or* a triangle to bang or hit
>
> ◆ a party horn *or* a recorder to blow
>
> ◆ a money box with coins in *or* a tambourine to shake.

Make a sound using one of the toys, and encourage your child to do the same. Then make two different sounds and encourage your child to copy them in the correct order. If your child is coping with these activities, make a sequence of three sounds and help him to repeat those in the correct order.

To start with, let your child see you making the different sounds.

❏ Sequencing actions

Make a series of different actions and encourage your child to copy your actions in the same order. Start with a sequence of two and gradually introduce new actions, for example:

◆ shake your hands in the air

◆ hide your hands behind your back

◆ put your hands on your hips.

❏ Sequencing everyday events

Draw simple pictures of everyday actions, for example:

◆ washing clothes (dirty clothes in a basket, a washing machine, clothes hanging on a washing line, ironing)

◆ making cakes or biscuits (ingredients, the mixture in the bowl, on the baking tray, in the oven, on the wire rack, etc)

◆ sequences in nature (a bird making a nest, eggs in the nest, eggs beginning to crack, bird bringing a worm for the chicks).

Talk to your child about each picture. Then cut out the pictures, mix them up and ask your child to help you rearrange them in the correct order.

You could also photograph your child at different times in the day, for example, waking up, brushing teeth, having breakfast, going to the park, playing in the garden, having dinner, going to sleep. Use the photos to talk about events in the past or print them and make a book or sort them into the right order.

❏ *Sequencing stories*

Look at picture books, or read favourite stories over and over again. Traditional stories are popular with young children, for example: *The Gingerbread Man, Goldilocks and the Three Bears, The Three Little Pigs* and *Three Billy Goats Gruff*. There are more examples in the resources section in the Appendix.

As your child becomes familiar with the story, encourage him to anticipate what will happen next before turning the page.

Draw simple pictures of the story. Mix up the pictures and ask your child to help you rearrange them in the correct order. If you have some old books, pictures can be cut out. You could also try making stick puppets of the characters in the book to act out the story.

Ⓟ You may photocopy this page for instructional use only © Charlotte Lynch & Julia Kidd, 2016 Speechmark

RECORD SHEET

Child's name: ....

An essential part of language learning involves remembering information which is taken in through the auditory and visual channels.

AIM OF ACTIVITIES	COMMENT AND DATE
VISUAL (p110) To develop visual memory skills: Kim's game, Animal hide-and-seek, Snap!, Matching pairs, Shopping game, Who's got the animal?, Changing places.	
Activities tried:	
SEQUENTIAL (p113) To develop sequential memory skills: Feed the monster, Washing line game, I went for a walk, I went shopping, Sequencing sounds, actions, everyday events and stories.	
Activities tried:	
AUDITORY (pp111, 112) To develop auditory memory skills: Shopping game, Who's got the animal?, Changing places.	
Activities tried:	

Ⓟ You may photocopy this page for instructional use only © Charlotte Lynch & Julia Kidd, 2016 Speechmark

Section 9

Early Words

Early Words

GENERAL POINTS

From the day they are born, babies are learning to communicate, first through their cries and the responses of people around them. Then they start to coo and babble and make the connection between their mouth movements, the sounds they make and the reaction they get from others. Often, children will make sounds that represent a familiar word but are not clear, for example, 'bor' for ball or 'din' for drink.

Early words are learned through copying and repetition. Children need to hear a word many times, and in many different situations, before they fully understand its meaning. They will understand more than they can say to begin with.

On page 131 a few of the most commonly learned first words are listed. Most of them are important and useful words for communication in the early years. There will be other words which individual children find interesting or useful and these should also be encouraged. Most words are best learned through spontaneous use during everyday events. Additional games can be played to reinforce children's understanding of these words.

Hints for encouraging early words

◆ Choose one or two words to focus on for a week, a month or as long as is necessary for your child. Choose words which your child will find useful or interesting. They may be words which your child is already trying to say.

◆ These words can be used repetitively, and in many different ways. The words should be used in short, simple sentences wherever possible, not on their own; for example, "Do you want a **biscuit**? Where are the **biscuits**? I've found them! Here's a **biscuit** for you. **Biscuit** – thank you, yum!"

◆ Use the words in everyday situations wherever possible.

◆ Give your child time to talk. Copy or extend any words he attempts and praise all of his efforts.

◆ Make sure that family and friends are aware of the words you are trying to encourage, so that they can help too.

◆ It is important not to spoil your child's enjoyment of a game by insisting on an attempt at the word.

◆ Offer choices, for example "Do you want juice or milk?"

◆ Use pictures, signs or gestures to offer choices.

Ⓟ You may photocopy this page for instructional use only © Charlotte Lynch & Julia Kidd, 2016

◆ Symbolic words are good to start with because they are easy sounds to say; for example, 'moo', 'beep beep', 'wheeee!'

◆ Set up situations such as deliberately giving a cup without a drink and waiting for your child to ask for drink, more or gone, etc. Model the request so that they can copy and use the early word.

◆ Look at familiar repetitive stories and leave pauses, waiting for your child to fill in the gaps; for example, 'Run, run as fast as you …, you can't catch me I'm the gingerbread …'. (There are suggestions for familiar repetitive stories in the resources section of the Appendix.)

Ⓟ You may photocopy this page for instructional use only © Charlotte Lynch & Julia Kidd, 2016 Speechmark

Lists of early words

Familiar names	Common objects		Social words	Action words
mummy	aeroplane	apple	hello	go
daddy	ball	orange	bye bye	fall
own name	boat	ears	please	up
man	book	eyes	thank you	stop
woman/lady	bus	hair	more	walk
boy	car	mouth	no	push
girl	teddy	nose	again	pull
baby	train	teeth		wash
	cat	cake		drink
	bird	biscuit		round and round
	dog	ice-cream		down
	duck	hat		run
	fish	coat		jump
	bag	shoes		sleep
	cup			(all) gone

Describing words	Pronouns	Symbolic words
big	me	beep beep
little	my	choo choo
hot	mine	quack quack
cold	you	moo
wet	yours	bang
noisy	your	boing
quiet		wheeee!
colours		pop!
		woof woof
		meow
		shhhh

P You may photocopy this page for instructional use only © Charlotte Lynch & Julia Kidd, 2016 Speechmark

Social words

ACTIVITIES

☐ *Hello/bye bye*

Toy telephone: talk into the phone, saying "Hello" and "Bye bye".

Glove puppets: make the puppets wave 'Hello' and 'Bye bye'.

Peek-a-boo games: hide and reappear, saying "Bye bye" and "Hello".

Mirror play: look in the mirror, saying "Hello" and "Bye bye".

Play shops: say "Hello" and "Bye bye" when the customer arrives and leaves.

☐ *More*

Playdough food and drink: give your child a little at a time, so that he is likely to ask for more.

Bubbles: encourage your child to say "More" before blowing bubbles again.

Building towers: give your child one brick at a time, and wait for an attempt at 'more' before giving him the next one.

Beach ball or balloon: blow it up a little at a time; stop and allow your child time to ask for 'more' before continuing.

Money box: give your child one coin at a time to put in the money box.

☐ *No*

Knocking coloured balls into holes: pretend to get it wrong (put the wrong colours in the holes).

Inset puzzles or posting boxes: try the above activity again. "Will it fit in there? No, I don't think so. What about this one? No!"

Hiding games: hide a small object in one hand. Your child should guess which hand it is in.

Lift-the-flap books: as you lift the flaps, say "Is it Spot the dog? No, it's the lion."

ⓟ You may photocopy this page for instructional use only © Charlotte Lynch & Julia Kidd, 2016 Speechmark

❏ *Again*

If your child is amused by something you do, and wants you to repeat it, encourage him to say "Again" before you do it. Try some of the following activities to get your child's interest:

◆ pop-up ball

◆ wind-up toy

◆ building up and knocking down towers

◆ tickling games

◆ letting the air burst out of a balloon.

Ⓟ You may photocopy this page for instructional use only © Charlotte Lynch & Julia Kidd, 2016 Speechmark

Action words

ACTIVITIES

☐ *(All) Gone*

Emphasise the word 'gone' whenever the toys disappear, for example:

◆ Post toys into a box with a hole in the top.

◆ Cover objects with a scarf or hide them under a pot.

◆ Hide finger puppets behind your back.

◆ Roll a ball across the table and into a tin.

☐ *Up/down*

Encourage the use of 'up' in everyday situations: *up* the stairs or steps; lifting your child *up*.

Toy slide or ladder and a person: make the person move up a step every time you or your child says "Up".

Pop-up rocket: encourage an attempt at 'up' before your child presses the button.

Jack-in-the-box: there are opportunities for both 'up' and 'down' with this toy.

Copying games: standing up/sitting down, arms up/arms down.

Rhymes: roly poly, roly poly, up up up.

Balloons: these can be used for both 'up' and 'down' either by letting air out of a balloon and letting it go, or by throwing a balloon up and watching it float down.

☐ *Stop*

Watch out for when the music and movement of these toys stop:

◆ spinners

◆ wind-up musical toy

◆ wind-up toy

◆ cars.

Ⓟ You may photocopy this page for instructional use only © Charlotte Lynch & Julia Kidd, 2016 Speechmark Ⓢ

Make a 'STOP' sign and play a game of stopping the traffic at pedestrian crossings, traffic lights, road junctions, and so on.

Round and round

Say "Round and round" with the movement of toys such as a roundabout, a spinning-top or a music box.

Draw circles round and round on a sheet of paper.

Play hospitals, putting on bandages, round and round the arm, leg or head.

Use rhymes: 'Round and round the garden, like a teddy bear'; 'The wheels on the bus go round and round'.

Go

Say "Go" before you:

◆ roll a ball down a tube or to each other

◆ release wind-up toys

◆ push a toy figure down a slide

◆ knock down a tower

◆ throw a brick into a box

◆ throw a ball at some skittles.

Push/pull

Push and pull bricks apart, making a big game of pushing and pulling.

Push pegs into a board and pull them out.

Thread beads on a string.

Push and pull a toy into and out of playdough or plasticine.

Pull and push wool through holes in sewing cards.

Pull pen caps off and push them back on.

Ⓟ You may photocopy this page for instructional use only © Charlotte Lynch & Julia Kidd, 2016 Speechmark

❏ *Jump/run/sleep*

Make a teddy, doll or favourite toy jump, run or sleep.

Make a glove puppet go to sleep and try to wake it up.

Make a toy jump on a pretend trampoline.

Jump into a hoop.

Hide under a blanket and pretend to go to sleep.

Play an action game where your child has to listen to your commands of run/jump/sleep and add other action words such as 'walk' or anything else.

Ⓟ You may photocopy this page for instructional use only © Charlotte Lynch & Julia Kidd, 2016 Speechmark

Describing words

ACTIVITIES

❏ Hot/cold

Everyday activities provide opportunities to use the words 'hot' and 'cold', for example:

◆ making jelly, ice cubes or ice lollies

◆ warning about hot water, tea, dinner or radiators.

❏ Wet

There are many everyday opportunities for using the word 'wet', for example:

◆ water play

◆ washing teddy's clothes

◆ hanging out the washing

◆ spilling a drink

◆ splashing in puddles

◆ wetting hair.

❏ Big/small

Sort big or small balls, toy animals or cars into boxes or large hoops.

Stories such as *Goldilocks and the Three Bears* and *Three Billy Goats Gruff* are useful for talking about big and small.

Cut out three different-sized arches in an old cardboard box: big, medium and small. Roll marbles across the table into the arches.

Remember to keep marbles out of the reach of very young children.

Pronouns

ACTIVITIES

❏ *Mine/yours*

'Snap!' playing cards: share out the cards using appropriate vocabulary, such as "This is yours. This is mine".

Lotto games: match the cards and talk about who each card belongs to; for example; "Is this yours? No, it's mine."

Share out toys or sweets.

Tea party with a tea set: give out and match different coloured cups and saucers.

Thread beads: each person can choose a different colour to make a necklace; for example, 'That's mine, it's a red one. Here's a blue one, this is yours."

❏ *My turn/your turn*

Take it in turns to:

- throw a bean bag into a bucket
- knock down skittles
- colour in part of a picture
- throw a dice
- make a plastic frog jump into a 'pond'.

❏ *Noisy/quiet*

Sort a mixture of noisy and quiet toys according to 'noisy' or 'quiet'; for example, lion, bear, monkey, drum versus mouse, sleeping baby, fish making a 'p-p-p' sound.

Use opportunities for noisy and quiet in everyday situations; for example, television or music, family members talking.

Whisper when a toy or a baby is 'asleep', and talk about being quiet. Make the toy or baby wake up because it is too noisy and talk about being noisy.

Put your hands over your ears for 'noisy' and a finger on your lips for 'quiet'.

Play musical instruments noisily and quietly.

Use animal pictures; for example, be loud like a lion and quiet like a mouse.

Ⓟ You may photocopy this page for instructional use only © Charlotte Lynch & Julia Kidd, 2016 Speechmark Ⓢ

❏ *Me/you*

Share out playing cards, or bricks, or sweets, saying "One for you and one for me."

Give each other toys or other objects, point to yourself or your child when you say 'me' and 'you': "That's for me. Here's one for you."

Roll a ball backwards and forwards to each other, using the opportunities for saying "You" and "Me".

Symbolic words

ACTIVITIES

☐ *Bang bang*

Bang pegs or balls into holes.

Bang two bricks together.

Bang a drum.

☐ *Beep beep*

Push a toy car along the table or floor.

Make the car disappear into a hole in a box.

Hide the car under a beaker and push it along.

Make a paper road for toy cars to travel on.

Push the car along your child's arm or into your pocket or up your sleeve.

☐ *Quack quack*

Play with plastic ducks in a bowl of water.

Make a cardboard duck stick puppet and make it pop up from under a table.

Make duck shadow puppets.

Feed the ducks.

Say the rhyme: 'Five little ducks went swimming one day'.

☐ *Boing/pop/bang!*

Bounce up and down.

Bounce a ball.

Make a springy toy bounce.

Blow bubbles and pop them.

Sing 'Ten fat sausages sizzling in the pan, one went POP! and the other went BANG!'

Bang bricks together.

Bang a drum.

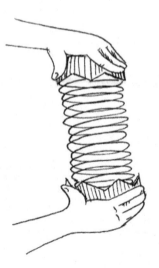

ℙ You may photocopy this page for instructional use only © Charlotte Lynch & Julia Kidd, 2016 Speechmark

Familiar names

ACTIVITIES

❏ *Mummy, Daddy and own name*

Turn-taking games: throwing a ball, blowing bubbles, sharing sweets or fruit.

Magazine pictures: find pictures of Mummy, Daddy and a child, and then sort them into different boxes.

Photographs: take photographs of family and close friends and stick them in a book, writing the names underneath. Look at the book frequently, and say the names.

Toy people and dolls: match them to pictures or members of the family, for example, mum, dad, grandma, baby.

Glove or finger puppets: play with man, woman, boy and girl puppets or draw faces on your fingers.

Make a lift-the-flap house, or draw a house, with people looking out of the windows.

Draw a picture of a bus, tractor or car and cut out faces from old photographs to stick in the driver's seat.

❏ *Man/woman/lady*

Put toy men or women in a bus or car: give your child one figure at a time.

Hide toy people in pots or tins.

Put a man or a woman on top of a tower.

Hide a man or a woman in one of your hands.

Draw pictures of men and women.

Common Objects

ACTIVITIES

❏ *Car*

Playing with toy cars in different ways will provide many opportunities for using the word, for example:

Create a toy garage (a simple one can be made by cutting out doors in an old cardboard box and colouring or painting it).

Sort cars into colours, sizes and shapes.

Make a car from building bricks.

Cut out magazine pictures of cars.

Roll cars down a slope or through a cardboard tube.

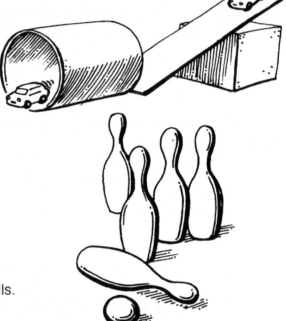

❏ *Ball*

Blow up a beach ball.

Play with skittles and a ball.

Make plasticine or playdough balls.

Blow table-tennis balls.

Roll balls backwards and forwards.

Draw, colour in and cut out pictures of balls.

Hide balls around the room.

❏ *Body parts: eyes/nose/mouth*

Point to your nose and then your child's nose.

Draw blank faces and add eyes, nose and mouth.

Make playdough faces.

Make a 'Mr Potato Head' toy.

Use dressing-up props: clown wigs/pop-out eyes/sunglasses.

❏ *My/your*

Point to my nose/your nose, my biscuit/your biscuit, my shoes/your shoes.

Play turn-taking games: my turn/your turn, my cup/your cup at a tea party with knife, fork, etc.

Share plastic or playdough food: your cake/my cake, etc.

Ⓟ You may photocopy this page for instructional use only © Charlotte Lynch & Julia Kidd, 2016 Speechmark Ⓢ

RECORD SHEET

Child's name: ....

Word(s) chosen: ....

DATE	GAME	IMITATION OF WORD (when your child copied you)	SPONTANEOUS USE OF WORD (when your child used the word on his own)	RESPONSE (what you said)

Ⓟ You may photocopy this page for instructional use only © Charlotte Lynch & Julia Kidd, 2016 Speechmark

RECORD SHEET

Child's name: ....

Children need to hear a word many times and in many different situations before they can begin to understand and use early words spontaneously.

AIM OF ACTIVITIES	COMMENT AND DATE
To develop comprehension. To encourage imitation of gestures and sounds. To use sounds in a meaningful way. To develop use of meaningful words. To record progress of emerging words and developing vocabulary.	
SOCIAL WORDS (p124) Hello, bye bye, more, no, again. Activities or words tried:	
ACTION WORDS (p126) (All) Gone, up, stop, round and round, go. Activities or words tried:	
DESCRIBING WORDS (p129) Hot, cold, wet, big, small. Activities or words tried:	

(continued)

Ⓟ You may photocopy this page for instructional use only © Charlotte Lynch & Julia Kidd, 2016 Speechmark

ACTIVITIES	COMMENT AND DATE
PRONOUNS (p130) Mine, yours, my turn, your turn. Activities or words tried:	
SYMBOLIC WORDS (p132) Bang bang, beep beep, quack quack. Activities or words tried:	
FAMILIAR NAMES (p133) Mummy, Daddy, own name, man/woman/lady. Activities or words tried:	
COMMON OBJECTS (p134) Car, ball. Activities or words tried:	

You may photocopy this page for instructional use only © Charlotte Lynch & Julia Kidd, 2016 Speechmark

Section 10

Putting Words Together

Putting Words Together

GENERAL POINTS

Once children have a vocabulary of approximately 50–100 words, they will start to put two or more words together. These two-word combinations may not be grammatically accurate to start with and the adult's role is important in interpreting the correct meaning and modelling the language with the correct grammar. For example, if the child says "Mummy work", the adult models by saying "Yes, mummy's going to work", or "No, mummy's not going to work today", or "Mummy's going to work later".

Children will learn best through simple language during everyday experiences. There are many opportunities to use two or more words together through everyday routines, such as 'shoes on', 'coat off', 'more drink', 'wash hands'.

Hints for encouraging two words together or more

◆ Listen and respond to your child's attempts to use words, so they know that you are interested in what they have to say.

◆ Repeat and extend your child's single words: for example, if he says 'ball', say "Yes, it's a *big ball*."

◆ Emphasise key words. Comment on what your child is doing and emphasise key words.

◆ Keep language simple and at your child's level.

◆ Look at books together and talk about what is happening in the pictures; for example, 'The *man's running*', 'The *dog* is *sleeping*'.

◆ Talk about objects and pictures in books, rather than just naming them; for example, 'Look, an *apple*. It's a *red apple*.'

◆ Sing nursery rhymes and leave pauses, waiting for your child to fill in the gaps; for example, 'Twinkle twinkle … (*little star*)'.

◆ Share family photographs and talk about what you are all doing in the pictures, what you are wearing, where you are, etc.

Children will learn best through what they are interested in, so there is no set order of which words to focus on first. However, social words such as 'bye', 'more', 'no' and 'please' are particularly good for combining early words, so they are a good starting point. Action words are particularly important because they are in every sentence. Action words such as 'gone', 'fall', 'jump' and 'run' also offer lots of opportunities to combine words in early two-word combinations. Some suggestions are made in this section for activities around putting words together, but these should not limit the words you use with your child. Model and extend correct forms; for example, where you want to focus on two words such as 'teddy gone', model this as 'Teddy's gone!' or 'Where's teddy gone? Teddy's hiding!'

ACTIVITIES

❏ *Bye/hello + object or person: Bye teddy, Hello daddy, Bye cat, Hello dog*

Everyday greetings provide many opportunities.

Play games with a pop-up toy.

Hide toy animals and glove puppets.

Pretend play with people or animals going into or coming out of houses, trains, animal homes, etc.

Play peek-a-boo games.

❏ *More + object: More biscuit, More orange, More cake*

Offer small pieces, such as an orange segment, and then use opportunities to model two words together: 'more orange?'

Do the same with toy bricks to make a tower, bubbles to ask for more, or beads to make a necklace.

❏ *No + object: No cake, No drink, No car, No fish*

Everyday situations provide many opportunities.

Laying the table: forget to add a spoon, cup, plate, fork, etc.

Tea parties: for example, one plate has cake on it, the other plate is empty.

Fishing games: 'fish' or 'no fish' on the line.

Use 'What's wrong?' pictures.

Hide small toys in boxes, leaving some empty: 'no car', 'no fish', etc.

❏ *Object + gone: Teddy gone, Ball gone, Car gone, Train gone, Apple all gone*

Everyday mealtimes provide many opportunities.

Roll balls to each other and under tables or chairs; hide them behind your back or under scarves.

Push a toy train through a tunnel, behind the sofa, or into a cardboard box.

🅟 You may photocopy this page for instructional use only © Charlotte Lynch & Julia Kidd, 2016 Speechmark

Play hide-and-seek with teddies or soft toys; hide them around the room or behind your back.

Post things in a post box or toy post boxes.

Post pictures, such as feeding the monster or the 'Greedy Gorilla' game (see the resources section in the Appendix).

❑ *Object + up/down: Ball up. Child's name up. Man up. Woman/lady down*

Throw balls up in the air or juggle with them.

Everyday experiences provide opportunities, for example: lifting your child up; commenting when he climbs up the stairs; going up and down the slide at the park.

Play with pop-up toys.

Pretend play; for example, toy people going up the steps and down the slide, or up and down ladders.

❑ *Pronoun or person + object: My ball. Your car. Baby's shoes. Mummy's bag. Daddy's book. Mummy's eyes. Daddy's nose. My mouth. Your hair*

Use everyday opportunities to talk about possessions around the house, clothes, toys, food, etc.

Have more than one ball or toy car and talk about who they belong to.

Parallel play with bouncing balls or pushing toy cars along a track.

Mirror play looking at faces.

Draw pictures of faces.

Ⓟ You may photocopy this page for instructional use only © Charlotte Lynch & Julia Kidd, 2016 Speechmark Ⓢ

❑ *Person or object + action: Baby sleep. Teddy jump. Fish round and round. Mummy wash*

Nearly all sentences need an action word, so there are lots of opportunities to bring them into your everyday talk by commenting on what you and your child are doing together.

Pretend play: baby or teddy can jump, fall, run, walk, sleep; the same with toy animals. Join in and make the toys do actions.

Look at books or photographs together and talk about what people are doing.

❑ *Describing word + object: Big plane. Little car. Noisy duck. Quiet baby. Wet hair. Cold ice-cream. Red bus*

Look at picture books together.

Sort objects or toy animals into sizes or colours.

Play matching games: for example, 'Goldilocks and the Three Bears'.

Use everyday experiences.

Play musical instruments to show 'noisy' and 'quiet'.

Ⓟ You may photocopy this page for instructional use only © Charlotte Lynch & Julia Kidd, 2016 Speechmark Ⓢ

RECORD SHEET

Child's name: ....

Children will learn best through simple language during everyday experiences. There are many opportunities to use two or more words together through everyday routines, such as 'shoes on', 'coat off', 'more drink', 'wash hands'.

AIM OF ACTIVITIES: To model and extend early words	**COMMENT AND DATE**
BYE/HELLO + OBJECT OR PERSON (p142) Bye teddy, Hello daddy, Bye cat, Hello dog Activities tried:	
MORE + OBJECT (p142) More biscuit, More orange, More cake Activities tried:	
NO + OBJECT (p142) No cake, No drink, No car, No fish Activities tried:	
OBJECT + GONE (p142) Teddy gone, Ball gone, Car gone, Train gone, Apple all gone Activities tried:	

continued

Ⓟ You may photocopy this page for instructional use only © Charlotte Lynch & Julia Kidd, 2016 Speechmark

AIM OF ACTIVITIES: To model and extend early words	COMMENT AND DATE
OBJECT + UP/DOWN (p143) Ball up, Child's name up, Man up, Woman/lady down	
Activities tried:	
PRONOUN OR PERSON + OBJECT (p143) My ball, Your car, Baby's shoes, Mummy's bag, Daddy's book ,Mummy's eyes, Daddy's nose, My mouth, Your hair	
Activities tried:	
PERSON OR OBJECT + ACTION (p144) Baby sleep, Teddy jump, Fish round and round, Mummy wash	
Activities tried:	
DESCRIBING WORD + OBJECT (p144) Big plane, Little car, Noisy duck, Quiet baby, Wet hair, Cold ice-cream, Red bus	
Activities tried:	

Ⓟ You may photocopy this page for instructional use only © Charlotte Lynch & Julia Kidd, 2016 Speechmark

RECORD SHEET

Child's name: ....

Word(s) chosen: ....

DATE	ACTIVITY	IMITATION OF WORDS (when your child copied you)	SPONTANEOUS USE OF WORDS (when your child used these words on his own)	RESPONSE (what you said)

Ⓟ You may photocopy this page for instructional use only © Charlotte Lynch & Julia Kidd, 2016 Speechmark

Appendix

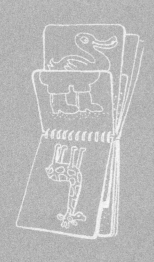

Further reading and useful websites

Linda Acredolo & Susan Goodwyn (2009) *Baby Signs: How to Talk with Your Baby before Your Baby Can Talk,* McGraw Hill Education, London.

Jean Cooper, Molly Moodley & Joan Reynell (1978) *Helping Language Development: A Development Programme for Children with Early Language Handicaps,* Edward Arnold, London.

Monica Devine (1991) *Baby Talk: The Art of Communicating with Infants and Toddlers,* Da Capo Press, Boston, MA.

Hazel Dewart & Susie Summers (1995) *Pragmatic Profile of Everyday Communication Skills in Children,* NFER Nelson, Slough.

Ann Locke (2013) *Teaching Speaking and Listening: One Step at a Time,* 2nd edn, Bloomsbury, London.

Useful websites

- ◆ www.dyspraxiafoundation.org.uk/.../Developmental_Verbal_Dyspraxia

- ◆ www.hanen.org: The Hanen Centre 'Helping You Help Children Communicate'

- ◆ www.hanen.org/Programs/For-parents/It-Takes-Two-to-Talk

- ◆ www.helpwithtalking.com

- ◆ www.ican.org.uk

- ◆ www.ndcs.org.uk

- ◆ www.ndp3.org/documents/ndp3-order-form.pdf

- ◆ www.rcslt.org

- ◆ www.speechmark.net/shop/early-skills-set-5-titles: Early Skills publications

- ◆ www.talkingpoint.org.uk: Talking Point 'Speech and Language in Children'

Resources and materials

Toys for encouraging vocalisations and early words

There are many reasonably priced sound-sensitive toys available on the high street, in catalogues and online, such as dancing flowers which move when you make a sound. These can be used to encourage vocalisations.

There are also many specialist sensory toys available from specialist toy shops or websites, for example:

◆ Fun and Achievement for People with Special Needs
 5–7 Severnside Business Park
 Stourport-on-Severn
 Worcestershire DY13 9HT, UK
 Website: specialneedstoys.com

Other toys and games include:

◆ echo mikes or 'Okideoke' (to record messages or sing along), from specialneedstoys.com

◆ kazoos (which require a vocalisation to get a sound)

◆ toobaloos (which you can talk into and get sound back into your ear)

◆ click clack car track
 (available from high street stores).

◆ Greedy Gorilla and other post-box games
 (available from www.orchardtoys.com/games).

Ⓟ You may photocopy this page for instructional use only © Charlotte Lynch & Julia Kidd, 2016 Speechmark

Mr Tongue story

This is a story about Mr Tongue who does different things, encouraging the child to copy tongue movements in an enjoyable way. Several stories are available to download free of charge, for example:

◆ *Mr Tongue's House,* adapted with permission from the story by E Love & S Reilly (1995) *A Sound Way. Phonological Awareness – Activities for Early Literacy,* Pearson, Melbourne.

Other stories are available online or for purchase, for example:

◆ *Mr Tongue* book from Winslow® Resources for Education, Health and Social Care: www.winslowresources.com/mr-tongue.html

Vowel cards

Pictures are used to represent vowels from a variety of different sources or programmes that suit the child being worked with and possibly match the pre-school, nursery or school approach to phonics. For example,

◆ Nuffield Dyspraxia Programme: www.ndp3.org

◆ *Bigmouth* apps: available from Vox Aux (www.voxaux.com)

◆ Jolly Phonics: jollylearning.co.uk/overview-about-jolly-phonics/

◆ *Cued Articulation* by Jane Passy: stasspublications.co.uk

◆ *Read Write Inc.* by Ruth Miskin: www.ruthmiskin.com/en/read-write-inc-programmes/phonics/

◆ *Communicate in Print* Widgit software is great for symbol support: www.widgit.com

◆ THRASS English Phonics: www.englishphonicschart.com

◆ Letterland characters: www.letterland.com › Shop

◆ Cued Speech Association: www.cuedspeech.co.uk

Other resources

◆ Ling-6 sounds flashcards are freely downloadable from the internet or at:

hope.cochlearamericas.com

www.advancedbionics.com

◆ Apps:

Ling sounds – *Auditory Verbal* by Melissa Essenburg (small charge)

Ling - 6 sound app for mobile phones which is free to download

Bla Bla – encourages vocalisations (free)

smartyearsapps.com – *Speechtrainer 3D* gives specific information regarding speech sounds and vowels (not free).

Below there are some suggestions for repetitive stories which are good for anticipating words and phrases.

◆ *The Gingerbread Man*: 'Run, run as fast as you can, you can't catch *me*, I'm the gingerbread *man*'.

◆ *The Three Little Pigs*: 'I'll huff and I'll puff and I'll *blow* your house down'.

◆ *Dear Zoo* by Rod Campbell (2009): 'I sent him *back*'.

◆ *Brown Bear Brown Bear* by Eric Carle (1995): 'Brown bear brown bear, what do you see? I see a *yellow duck* looking at *me*'.

◆ *The Very Hungry Caterpillar* by Eric Carle (1981): 'He ate through five *oranges*, but he was still *hungry*'.

◆ *The Very Busy Spider* by Eric Carle (1995): 'She was very busy spinning her *web*'.

◆ *One, Two, Three, JUMP!* by Penelope Lively (1999): this is good for 'One, two, three, JUMP!' activities.

◆ *Where's My Teddy?* by Jez Alborough (1994): this is good for anticipating rhymes.

◆ *This is the Bear* by Sarah Hayes and Helen Craig (2003): this is good for anticipating rhymes.

ⓟ You may photocopy this page for instructional use only © Charlotte Lynch & Julia Kidd, 2016

◆ *Peace at Last* by Jill Murphy (2013): this is great for symbolic sounds such as 'tick-tock', 'drip-drip', etc.

◆ *Whatever Next?* by Jill Murphy (2007): this is great for symbolic sounds (WHOOSH!, UP!), early words and acting out with props.

◆ *Where is Maisy?* by Lucy Collins (2010): a lift-the-flap book for 'No, not here!'

◆ *Oh Dear!* by Rod Campbell (2009): a lift-the-flap book for 'Oh dear!'

◆ *Here's Buster but Where's Teddy?* by Rod Campbell (2000): this is good for 'Where?' and 'Here!'

◆ *I Went Walking* by Sue Williams, illustrated by Julie Vivas (1997): this is good for animals and noises and filling in gaps for 'what did you see?' and 'looking at me'.

Services for deaf children

◆ The Elizabeth Foundation for deaf children charity is a pre-school service which runs a national home learning and support programme for parents of pre-school deaf children:

The Elizabeth Foundation Trust for Deaf Children
Southwick Hill Road
Portsmouth PO6 3LL, UK
Website: elizabeth-foundation.org

◆ DASL skills – Success for Kids with Hearing Loss: *The Developmental Approach to Successful Listening II* is a sequential, step-by-step listening program to help hearing impaired children and adults. Available at: successforkidswithhearingloss.com

Ⓟ You may photocopy this page for instructional use only © Charlotte Lynch & Julia Kidd, 2016 Speechmark 163

Support training programme for parents and support staff

INTRODUCTION

This six-session programme can be used with parents, carers or support staff as a series of training workshops. It is based on the activities and information in this book and will help to give those involved a better understanding of early communication skills, and the confidence to extend and develop a child's language.

Each session is designed to last about one hour but they could be longer, depending on the number of activities chosen.

You may photocopy this page for instructional use only © Charlotte Lynch & Julia Kidd, 2016 Speechmark

SUPPORT SESSION 1: INTRODUCTION AND EYE CONTACT

Learning outcomes

1 To be aware of the importance of eye contact in early communication.

2 To learn ways of encouraging better eye contact.

3 To learn some practical activities for improving eye contact.

Handouts

Any or all of the following pages can be photocopied.

p7: Hints for parents

p11: Eye contact general points

p12: Eye contact activity suggestions

p30: Record sheet

Resources

◆ An object of interest or a photograph to talk about

◆ Feathers, scarves, bubbles, a ball, or any toys to encourage eye contact

◆ Emotions cards and phrases

◆ Flipchart and marker pen

Activities

1 Talk about pre-verbal skills. Ask parents to think about how babies and young children are communicating before they speak. Thinking about their own children, get them to talk to a partner about what their children are doing at the moment. How do they communicate if they are hungry, excited, sad, happy, frustrated?

Give them two minutes to discuss and then feed back to the group. Write a list of communication skills on a flipchart, eg looking, smiling, laughing, shaking or moving legs and arms, jumping up and down, shouting, snatching, throwing, crying. Emphasise that these are all important for early communication, and the parents' role in building on these communication attempts is crucial.

2 Discuss the general points of eye contact. Set up a role play with you and a volunteer parent. Person A talks about their holiday or their family. Person B looks around the room and does not make eye contact with person A. Discuss how you both feel. Does the group have any comments about the communication they observed?

3   Choose an object of interest that you want to talk about: a book, a photo, an ornament, etc. Talk to another volunteer parent and look at the object together. Ask the group to comment on what both people in the conversation did, eg looked together at it, commented together, took turns, copied ways of holding it, etc. These are all important in communication. (Note: if the child is deaf, it is very important that he is looking at what you are talking or signing about.)

4   Emotions pictures. Give parents an emotion picture to act out with a different partner (see the examples on page 167). Can the partner guess what emotion it is? Discuss the importance of facial expression and varied intonation in getting the child's attention and eye contact. Practise saying phrases: 'Wow!', 'Oh no!', 'Bye!', 'Yum!' (see below) Is it possible to say these words without expression? Does the way you say them change the meaning? Are they effective without eye contact?

    Discuss ways of attracting your child's attention by holding objects near to your face, putting them on your head or hiding them behind your back. Discuss how you can wait a few seconds for eye contact before giving your child what they need. Demonstrate with a ball, throwing it to the parents.

5   Try out some activities and be aware of the role of eye contact, and how to expect eye contact before continuing play with feathers, scarves or bubbles.

    Give parents a record sheet and an idea to try at home which they think their child might like. Ask them to try it out and share with the group in the next session.

Words and phrases to say with and without expression

Wow!	Oh no!	Yum!
Bye!	No!	Yes!
Wait!	Stop it!	Give it to me!

You may photocopy this page for instructional use only © Charlotte Lynch & Julia Kidd, 2016 Speechmark

Emotions

happy   sad

surprised   scared

worried   cross

P You may photocopy this page for instructional use only © Charlotte Lynch & Julia Kidd, 2016 Speechmark

SUPPORT SESSION 2: ATTENTION

Learning outcomes

1   To understand what is meant by attention.

2   To learn ways of improving attention.

3   To learn some practical activities for improving attention.

Handouts

Any or all of the following pages can be photocopied.

p8: Improving communication

p15: Attention general points

pp16–19: Attention activity suggestions

p30: Record sheet

Resources

◆   Homemade playdough or equipment to make – or demonstrate how to make – playdough in the session

◆   Story box, story sack or nursery rhyme props or puppets

◆   Paper and pencils or crayons

◆   Any activity props such as bricks, balls, posting boxes, balloons, puzzles

Activities

1   Talk about how attention is important for communication and listening. Ask parents to discuss with a partner how long their child attends to one activity and what is their favourite activity or toy. What might be the barriers to paying attention, eg lots of toys out, television or other distractions?

2   Discuss the general points of attention and how to add surprise to games.

3   Look at an example of story sack or nursery rhyme props to demonstrate how interest in a book can be extended. Get parents to use paper and pencils to extend interest in nursery rhymes or stories or make a story sack. Choose a nursery rhyme such as 'Humpty Dumpty' and props such as a Humpty toy, brick or box to make a wall, toy horses and figures, drawing pictures of Humpty, etc.

4   Demonstrate making homemade playdough (see the recipe on page 169), or bring in some coloured playdough, and get parents to try different ways of playing with it.

ℙ You may photocopy this page for instructional use only © Charlotte Lynch & Julia Kidd, 2016 Speechmark

5 Parents choose a toy in pairs and discuss how many different ways they can think of to play with it. Then share ideas with the group.

6 Give parents a record sheet and get them to think of different ways to play with a favourite toy at home. The group can support each other with ideas. Ask them to try it out and share with the group at the next session. They can bring a photograph on their mobile phone if they like.

HOW TO MAKE HOMEMADE PLAYDOUGH

Ingredients

One cup of plain flour

Half a cup of salt

Two teaspoons of cream of tartar

One tablespoon of oil

Few drops of food colouring

Method

◆ Mix all of the ingredients in a saucepan and put it on a low heat.

◆ Stir continual with a wooden spoon for a few minutes until smooth and the dough comes away from side of the pan.

◆ Remove the dough and put the pan to soak in water immediately.

◆ Knead the dough for a few minutes.

◆ Use the dough when cooled and store it in an airtight container.

SUPPORT SESSION 3: COPYING AND TURN TAKING

Learning outcomes

1   To raise awareness of the role of copying and turn taking in early communication.

2   To learn how to improve copying and turn-taking skills.

3   To learn some practical ways of encouraging turn taking and copying.

Handouts

Any or all of the following pages can be photocopied.

p22: Copying: General points

p26: Turn taking: General points

pp23/25: Copying activity suggestions

pp27/29: Turn-taking activity suggestions

p30: Record sheet

p172: My turn/your turn cards

Resources

◆   Egg timer or clock timer

◆   Mirror, teddy or doll, plastic rings on a stick, toy bricks or hats

◆   Selection of books with songs and rhymes

◆   Short video clip of adult and child taking turns and copying babble or noises such as 'funny baby copying her mum' or 'talking twin babies' (there are several on YouTube).

Activities

1   Talk about how copying and turn taking is important for the development of communication skills. Watch a short video clip of a parent and child or two toddlers babbling together and taking turns. Ask parents to observe all of the skills such as eye contact, turn taking and copying. Watch how the people in the video take turns and copy each other's facial expressions or actions.

2   Discuss the general points of copying (p22) and how to extend children's noises and babble, through repeating and modelling their speech, and commenting on what they do. Talk about how you can add language to comment on what you are doing. Give two toy bricks or a hat to each parent. Get them to copy what the other does in pairs. Then ask parents to suggest what language they can add to the activity. For example,

Ⓟ You may photocopy this page for instructional use only © Charlotte Lynch & Julia Kidd, 2016

for bricks: *bang bang, oh that's noisy, one two three, quietly, where's it gone? Up high.* Or for hat: *my hat, put it on your head, too big, peek-a-boo,* etc.

Ask a parent to volunteer to role play with you, or another parent, copying sounds while looking in a mirror.

Copy and extend the sounds they make and discuss how parents attach meaning to early sounds.

Ask the parents to discuss with a partner, or share with the group, how they can include their children in copying everyday routines.

3   Discuss the general points of turn taking (p26). Show how a timer can be used to encourage older children to share and take turns. How can parents get young children to give and take with toys? Set up a role play with person A being a toddler who is reluctant to give a toy back. Demonstrate how you can offer another toy in exchange. Demonstrate with rings on a stick or another toy how you could take turns and copy play.

4   Demonstrate 'Simon says' or 'Follow my leader'. Role play taking turns at being the leader. Use 'my turn/your turn' visual prompts (see the examples on page 172). Talk about sharing roles; for example, one child rolls out the pastry and the other cuts out shapes.

5   Give parents a record sheet and get them to choose a copying or turn-taking game that their child will enjoy. Ask them to try it out and share with the group in the next session.

My Turn/Your Turn Cards

Ⓟ You may photocopy this page for instructional use only © Charlotte Lynch & Julia Kidd, 2016 Speechmark Ⓢ

SUPPORT SESSION 4: LANGUAGE, PLAY AND AUDITORY/VISUAL MEMORY

Learning outcomes

1   To understand the role of play and auditory/visual memory in developing language.

2   To learn how to encourage language through play.

3   To learn some practical ways of improving memory for spoken language.

Handouts

Any or all of the following pages can be photocopied.

pp33–44: Language and play general points

p117: Auditory and visual memory general points

pp35–44: Language and play activity suggestions

pp118–124: Auditory and visual memory activity suggestions

p45: Language and play record sheet

p125: Auditory and visual memory record sheet

Resources

◆   Boxes of different sizes

◆   Pictures and objects for 'Kim's game'

◆   Story sequence pictures

◆   'Greedy Gorilla' game, or a 'monster' box and pictures of insects or animals, or a washing line, pegs and pictures.

Activities

1   Discuss different types of play and how they are important for language development and imaginative thinking. Ask parents what their child enjoys doing most and match this to the different types of play.

2   Ask parents to discuss with a partner how their child wants to be, or could be, involved in everyday routines (see the examples below). What kind of everyday objects do they like to explore? This may include things they are not meant to play with. Share ideas with the group.

Bring in some large boxes. How can these be used to develop imaginary play and language? For example, as story boxes, posting boxes, or houses/trains/spaceships for imaginary play.

3   Play a group auditory and visual memory game, such as 'Kim's game' (see page 118). Consider how you are using auditory and visual memory to help organise and remember the information. Are people visual or auditory learners? Or do they need to feel and hold the objects or pictures to help them remember?

4   Talk through the different games to encourage auditory and visual memory (page 118 in section 8). Divide parents into pairs or groups and give them one game to play, then feed back to the group. Draw some simple pictures of everyday events and talk about the language that goes with them. Give parents sequence pictures of a well-known story (see the example on pages 175 and 176). Ask them to put the pictures in the right order. Think about the language they use.

5   Ask parents to decide on one activity to try out before the next session and record this on a record sheet to share with the group.

Ⓟ You may photocopy this page for instructional use only © Charlotte Lynch & Julia Kidd, 2016 Speechmark

Example 1 picture sequence

℗ You may photocopy this page for instructional use only © Charlotte Lynch & Julia Kidd, 2016 Speechmark

Example 2 picture sequence

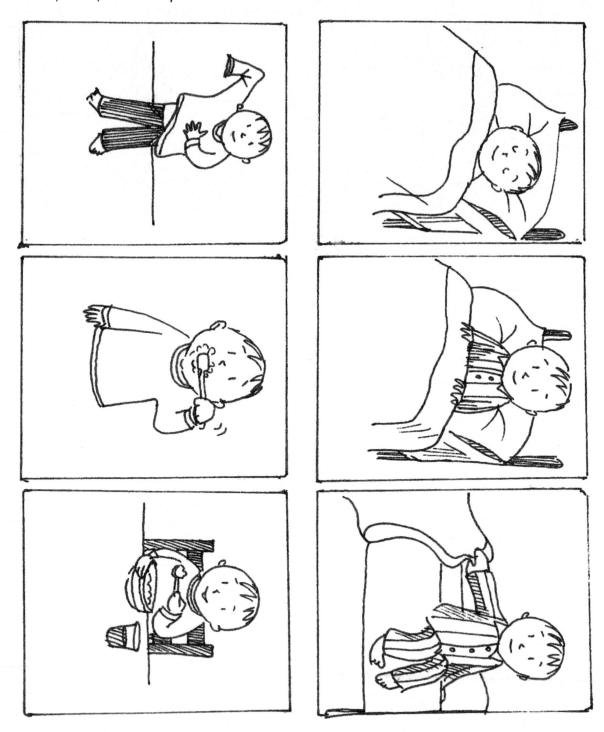

Ⓟ You may photocopy this page for instructional use only © Charlotte Lynch & Julia Kidd, 2016 Speechmark

SUPPORT SESSION 5: EARLY LISTENING AND VOCALISATIONS

Learning outcomes

1   To recognise how babies and young children show that they have heard a sound.

2   To know how to improve awareness of sound and voice.

3   To know how to extend vocalisations into a conversation.

Handouts

Any or all of the following pages can be photocopied.

p49: Awareness of sound general points

p61: Awareness of voice general points

p77: Vocalisations general points

pp51–7: Awareness of sound activity suggestions

pp62–71: Awareness of voice activity suggestions

pp78–80: Vocalisations activity suggestions

p52: 'Sounds my child responds to' record sheet

p81: Vocalisations, 'Sounds my child makes' record sheet

p50: Tips on keeping in hearing aids and cochlear implants

Resources

◆   Old biscuit tin plus uncooked rice and wooden spoon, musical balloons, homemade sound shakers

◆   Old objects to make shakers from, eg plastic containers and dried pasta, peas or rice

◆   'Sound box' of symbolic sounds toys

◆   'Row the boat' song words

◆   Glove puppets

Activities

1   Discuss how many babies like the sound of a human voice best. Deaf children may not be aware of speech sounds without their hearing aids or cochlear implants, so it is important for them to wear their equipment. Discuss keeping in hearing aids or cochlear implants, if relevant (p50).

2   Brainstorm some common sounds around the house or garden which children may respond to: washing machine, doors banging, footsteps, letters being posted through the front door, etc. Discuss how you can draw attention to the sounds and use language together to talk about them.

Look at some toys which use all of the senses to improve awareness of sound, for example: things to bang, blow, or shake (p51).

Make some sound-shakers from tins and leave some of them empty to show the difference between sound and silence (p46). Play 'Wake up teddy' to a sound signal (p55). Hide a musical toy in the room and ask a parent to volunteer to locate the sound (p57).

Discuss what is meant by symbolic sounds and make a list of ones that parents may use, such as 'ahhh', 'mmmm', 'shhh'.

3   Have a 'sound box' of toys or objects with associated symbolic sounds (eg tractor for 'brum brum', ball for 'boing boing') and ask parents to think of more sound toys which they could add to the box. Use the toys to show 'stop/start' with your voice, (eg voice makes a noise when a toy car is pushed along and stops when the car stops).

Choose a nursery rhyme and show how you can encourage children to anticipate sounds by leaving a pause, eg for 'Row the boat': "If you see a crocodile, don't forget to scream … AHHHHH!" (see page opposite).

4   Talk about vocal play and the importance of babble. Discuss activities which make children particularly vocal.

5   Talk about repeating and extending vocalisations, eg child says "ma" and parent extends this to "Mummy, you saying hello to mummy?" Demonstrate some of the games from the awareness of sound section; for example, how can glove puppets be used to encourage children to vocalise?

6   Ask parents to record either the sounds their child responds to or the sounds their child makes on the record sheet and bring it to share with the group in the next session.

You may photocopy this page for instructional use only © Charlotte Lynch & Julia Kidd, 2016   Speechmark

Row, row, row your boat,

Gently down the stream,

Merrily, merrily, merrily, merrily,

Life is but a dream.

Row, row, row your boat,

Gently down the stream,

If you see a crocodile,

Don't forget to scream … AHHHHH!

Ⓟ You may photocopy this page for instructional use only © Charlotte Lynch & Julia Kidd, 2016   Speechmark Ⓢ

SUPPORT SESSION 6: EARLY WORDS AND PUTTING WORDS TOGETHER

Learning outcomes

1   To recognise the stages of communication leading to early first words.

2   To know how to encourage early words through play.

3   To be aware of how to extend early words through everyday routines.

Handouts

Any or all of the following pages can be photocopied.

p129: Early words general points

p149: Putting words together general points

p131: Lists of early words

pp132–42: Early words activity suggestions

p150: Putting words together activity suggestions

pp143–5: Early words record sheets

pp153–5: Putting words together record sheets

Resources

◆   List of early words, early words cards

◆   Playdough, bubbles, towers, balloons

◆   Paper and pens

◆   Simple picture books

◆   'Bye/hello + object or person' activity resources: pop-up toys, toy animals, glove puppets, pretend people, scarves.

Activities

1   Ask parents to discuss with a partner, or in the group, how their child communicates. Do they know their child's first words or older siblings' first words? What are common first words? Look at the lists of early words. Discuss how symbolic words (such as 'moo', 'ahhhh', 'oooooh', 'wheeee!') are easier words to say because there are fewer consonants. How do adults talk to babies and young children?
For example, a sing-song voice which holds their attention, repetition and 'silly talk'.

Ⓟ You may photocopy this page for instructional use only © Charlotte Lynch & Julia Kidd, 2016 Speechmark

2   Give parents an early words card (see the examples on p174). Ask them to discuss it in a pair and write down how they could emphasise this word in a simple phrase or sentence. For example, for biscuit: 'Do you want a biscuit? Where are the biscuits? I've found the biscuits! Here's a biscuit for you. Biscuit … thank you, yum!' Choose some of the early words activities, for example 'more', and demonstrate through role play how you can create opportunities for children to make an attempt at the word 'more' by playing with playdough, bubbles, towers, balloons, etc.

3   Ask parents if they can think of ways of using the same toys they used for 'more' to encourage early words like 'mummy', 'daddy' and the child's own name. Demonstrate how you can draw a picture of a bus or a house and add the faces of family members to talk about.

4   Look at picture books. Can parents think of comments on a book which involve more than one word? Make a list of possible adult input, for example: it's a **ball**, it's a **big ball**, it's a **big bouncy ball**, it's like **your ball** in the garden, it's a **red ball**. Talk about always being one step ahead, keeping language simple, but one step ahead of the child, to model and extend language. Look at a more detailed picture book and show how you can model verbs such as 'the **man** is **running**', the **dog** is **sleeping**'. Try one of the activities from Section 10 *Putting Words Together*, eg 'Bye/hello + object or person'.

5   Think about examples of language you can use through everyday routines such as getting dressed or mealtimes: 'shoes on', 'coat off', 'more drink', 'wash hands', etc. Give parents a record sheet of early words or putting words together.

You may photocopy this page for instructional use only © Charlotte Lynch & Julia Kidd, 2016 Speechmark

Early words cards

more	**no**
bye	**gone**
fall	**up**
car	**ball**
please	**mummy/daddy/ own name**
teddy	**fish**

Ⓟ You may photocopy this page for instructional use only © Charlotte Lynch & Julia Kidd, 2016   Speechmark

CPSIA information can be obtained
at www.ICGtesting.com
Printed in the USA
LVOW06s1610130317
527032LV00009B/654/P

9 781911 186267